Nadja-Christina Schneider
Fritzi-Marie Titzmann [eds.]

Family Norms and Images in Transition

Contemporary Negotiations of Reproductive Labor,
Love and Relationships in India

 **Nomos**

Die Deutsche Nationalbibliothek lists this publication in the
Deutsche Nationalbibliografie; detailed bibliographic data
is available in the Internet at http://dnb.d-nb.de

ISBN   978-3-8487-5225-6 (Print)
          978-3-8452-9405-6 (ePDF)

British Library Cataloguing-in-Publication Data
A catalogue record for this book is available from the British Library.

ISBN   978-3-8487-5225-6 (Print)
          978-3-8452-9405-6 (ePDF)

Library of Congress Cataloging-in-Publication Data
Schneider, Nadja-Christina / Titzmann, Fritzi-Marie (eds.)
Family Norms and Images in Transition
Contemporary Negotiations of Reproductive Labor, Love and Relationships in India
Nadja-Christina Schneider / Fritzi-Marie Titzmann
113 pp.
Includes bibliographic references.

ISBN   978-3-8487-5225-6 (Print)
          978-3-8452-9405-6 (ePDF)

Onlineversion
Nomos eLibrary

1st Edition 2020
© Nomos Verlagsgesellschaft, Baden-Baden, Germany 2020. Printed and bound in
Germany.

Contents

Introduction: Family Norms and Images in Transition. Contemporary Negotiations of Reproductive Labor, Love and Relationships in India

Fritzi-Marie Titzmann & Nadja-Christina Schneider

The family occupies a pivotal space in the reality and imagination of societies and individuals. Within the Indian context, the family holds a peculiar ideological symbolism in the form of a strong nexus of so-called family values and nationalism. Ever since attempts from the 19th century onwards to withstand challenges of colonial dominance and a subsequent erasure of indigenous culture and 'tradition', the private space of the home and family has symbolized a refuge of – however defined – 'Indianness' and an emerging national identity. While gendered norms and images change with political circumstances, the family remains a strong and highly contested symbol of national identity. The debate over meaning, acceptable family forms and role models is shaped by, and shapes, social, political, and technological changes. In contemporary India, the politics of post-liberalisation set the conditions for the envisioning, re-assessment, and propagation of family norms, in particular concerning representations of desirable and non-desirable relationships and the roles ascribed to men and women within the family and greater society respectively. Particularly with the rise of political Hinduism, the inherent tensions and contradictions between cultural-nationalist notions of the 'Indian family' and the multiple lived realities and ways of 'doing' family or kinship became more apparent. As is well known, a conservative, religiously defined and hierarchically structured family ideal is an integral component of the Hindutva ideology. Nonetheless, under Prime Minister Narendra Modi's Hindu nationalist government (since 2014), India witnessed amendments to existing laws and enactment of new laws that provide support to women, such as the Maternity Benefit (Amendment) Act 2017 or the initiative *Beti Bachao Beti Padhao* [Save the Daughter, Educate the Daughter]. The political cooptation by the Hindu Right of discourses about 'gender justice' and 'female empowerment' has been mentioned and critiqued in feminist research but has hardly been a research objective itself.

Being largely dominated by a patriarchal lineage and family system, Indian society is witnessing changes as becomes evident in the increasing participation of women in the work force, the rise of a global youth culture that shapes the experience of new intimacies and media-related narratives of love and companionship. Technological innovation and increasing digitization do not only render new opportunities to forge relationships but also radically alter existing notions of parenthood, kinship and family. Assisted reproductive technologies, such as sperm donation, in-vitro fertilization or gestational surrogacy, allow for family formations of various kinds and with heterogenous actors, as becomes evident with newly coined terms like co-parenting, split parenthood or multi-parenthood. All over the world, the question what makes a family is currently being renegotiated and challenged by changing media representations, legal conceptualizations as well as social discourses and practices.

While 'alternative family models' can be said to have been a lived reality in India much earlier, it is interesting to note that they are now increasingly visually represented, for instance, in commercial advertising, literature or popular Hindi cinema. Accordingly, images of the family are highly contested on political, legal and media levels and these negotiation processes reveal contradictions, resistances, as well as continuities. In contrast to a substantial body of literature on the role of women within family and society, on marriage, and the construction of the ideal Indian family, other areas in family research are highly under-represented and show urgent research desiderate. All chapters in this volume provide insights into hitherto marginal aspects, but further fields of inquiry from normative and non-normative perspectives should encompass studies on singles and single parents, on disabilities, non-heteronormative families, and perhaps also a stronger focus on contested masculinity and male family members, as well as on ageing and on childhood.

In this volume, we attempt to widen the horizon and look at various shifts, ruptures and continuities in representations of contemporary Indian families from a media perspective. The medialization of family norms and images as well as the nature of romantic relationships constitutes our central approach that connects the different discussions in the chapters. The contributions analyze documentary and feature films, promotional material, such as television commercials, visual campaigns, and the usage of new media technologies in communication. This volume initiates a dialogue between research on normative national visions of family and parenthood (see Titzmann in this volume) and non-normative families, as represented in documentary images and feature films on assisted reproductive technologies (see both chapters by Schneider in this volume) or in discussing familial conflict in mainstream Hindi cinema (see Bhandari in this volume). Internet-based applications and the recent smartphone revolution have radically altered negotiations of romantic relationships in contemporary India (see Strulik in this volume). By including perspectives on the pre-marriage stage of life, we look at visualizations of familial change ranging from split motherhood, new fatherhood, and dysfunctional families to intergenerational relationships.

In an ever-changing world, the family continues to hold a dual function of simultaneously symbolizing persistence and transformation. While the idea of the family as such will outlast political and social upheavals on global and local levels, the forms and ways of doing family and kinship will be further differentiated, contested and re-altered. Conceptualized as part of a larger discourse on family and social change, this book thus aims at contributing to an understanding of the current – ideological and lived – realities of the Indian family within the complex dynamics of continuity and change.

Chapter 1: Reframing Indian Fatherhood: Manhood, Responsibility and Patriarchal Hegemony

Fritzi-Marie Titzmann

Introduction

The Bharatiya Janata Party (BJP) under Prime Minister Narendra Modi has been ruling India since 2014. Ideologically, the BJP belongs to the Hindu right-wing spectrum and hence represents a conservative, religious, and hierarchically structured family ideal. The Modi government's first term (2014-19) already indicated an increasingly repressive political climate that targeted the opposition in general, Human and Women's Rights activists, marginalized groups such as Dalits and Muslims, as well as left intellectual individuals and groups in particular. Right after their coming into power, predictions about the party's governing style differed from politically moderate to expecting a rapid development towards a Hindu chauvinist, anti-minority, authoritarian state. The former aggression was attributed to the purpose of winning the election battle.

When it comes to the question of gender equality and attitudes towards family politics, the BJP's positions are very ambiguous. On the one hand, the place reserved for women within Hindu right-wing ideology is demarcated clearly as inferior and located within the private sphere of home and family. On the other hand, as Poggendorf-Kakar (2003) has pointed out, the female Hindu goddess and the women warriors fighting for a resurrected Hindu nation are equally strong iconic figures. Interestingly, this ambiguity permeates the contemporary discourse on gender and family politics, too. The current BJP government initiated bills and campaigns within its first five years of power (2014-19) that can be interpreted as tools towards a more gender-just image of the Indian family. For instance, the BJP government propagates education and respect for daughters with its campaign *Beti Bachao Beti Padhao* [Save the daughter, educate the daughter] (BBBP). It further strengthens an entitlement to paid maternity leave with the *Maternity Benefit (Amendment) Act 2017* and has fostered a national midwifery-training program since December 2018 in order to improve Indian women's birth experiences and lower the maternal mortality rate. In 2015, Modi emphatically endorsed a small grassroots campaign from Haryana and made *#SelfieWithDaughter* first a national, and consequentially an international success. The campaign embodies a remarkable trend of focusing on girls as India's potential future. Apart from strengthening maternal health, the emphasis on positive father-daughter relationships represents a novel trajectory of family ideology.

The government itself explains its interest in taking up such initiatives not with an endorsement of social change as such but grounds its approach in a rhetoric of social and economic progress or development. As stated in the *Annual Report on Family Planning*, a desirable decline in the national birth rate facilitates demographic stabilization, »which in turn spurs the economic and social progress« (MoHFW Annual Report 2017-18: 86). The Hindi term *vikaas* (development) featured prominently in Modi's 2014 election campaign.[1] It is thus questionable whether the intention is one of gender justice or an attempt to define the development of the family in rather hegemonic terms.

This chapter interrogates possible renegotiations of hegemonic and patriarchal gender roles of parenting within the context of this recent reorientation of gender and family politics towards a stronger emphasis on initiatives in terms of gender mainstreaming. It does so by analyzing two notable campaigns that are either directly state-sponsored or officially promoted by members of the BJP government:

1. A multimedia campaign initiated by the Ministry of Health and Family Welfare (MoHFW) in the context of the Family Planning Program which prioritizes »Mardangi [Hindi: manhood] and the involvement of men« (MoHFW Annual Report 2017-18: 93) among its prime themes.
2. The #SelfieWithDaughter campaign, which was initially a local intervention by an individual but later on endorsed officially by Prime Minister Narendra Modi.

The following analysis of the campaigns is also an interrogation of contested notions of gender justice in contemporary India, since

---

1   One of his election slogans was *sabka saath, sabka vikaas* (literally in Hindi: Everyone's support, everyone's development). Narendra Modi's official website translates the slogan into »Collective efforts, inclusive growth«. See: https://www.narendramodi.in/sabka-saath-sabkavikas-collective-efforts-inclusive-growth-3159 (last accessed October 24, 2019).

#SelfieWithDaughter in particular drew a lot of criticism and thereby generated a heated controversy. This chapter juxtaposes the ideological trope of men as driving progress and development, especially in the context of gender and family relations, with critical arguments that locate the unchanged positioning of women as dependent daughters within the context of patriarchal structures that restrict women's individual subjectivity and agency (Hussain 2015, Phadke 2007).

I argue that the strategies of both, the MoHFW campaign and #SelfieWithDaughter, in similar ways aim at reframing Indian manhood[2] in a positive light by associating it with progress and familial responsibility, which in turn reflect on the image of the Indian nation itself. The current Hindu right wing government projects a certain vision of ideal Indian manhood, which relates to two 'new' role models within the family: the responsible and emancipated husband and the responsible and caring father. Contrary to the 'progressive' impression these campaigns leave at first view, I suggest they do not contribute towards challenging hegemonic masculinity in the Indian context but rather perpetuate patriarchal structures by concealing the existing power relations with superficial aspects of equality and female empowerment.

The following section explores trajectories of 'new' Indian fatherhood that prepare the ground for an analysis of the success and controversies generated by #SelfieWithDaughter. The MoHFW campaign did, to my knowledge, not cause comparable debates but serves as a paradigmatic example of the state's visualization of ideal male (and female) behavior with regard to family planning by highlighting responsibility and an awareness of national visions of health and progressiveness.

Towards 'New' Indian Fatherhood?

Despite a growing popularity of masculinity studies in the South Asian context, substantial research on contemporary fatherhood and images of Indian fathers beyond the discussion of changing 'traditional' gender roles and labor division within the family[3] is sparse. The discussion following the so-

---

2   The author is aware of the existence of multiple masculinities, which include queer, homosexual and other marginalized masculinities in South Asia. Nevertheless, this paper focuses on the construction of heterosexual masculinity in the normative discourse of the Indian state.

3   For example, Pernau, Ahmed & Reifeld 2003, Mines & Lamb 2002.

called Delhi Gang Rape Case (Schneider & Titzmann 2014) contributed to a serious inquiry into hegemonic masculinity and the 'right' upbringing of boys.[4] Nevertheless, in comparison to the extensive debate on the trope of »Mother India«, that dominates motherhood as a religious-cultural category[5], fatherhood as an object of academic study remains neglected. Psychologically oriented studies by Sriram (2019, 2011) and Saraff & Srivastava (2008) are an exception.

Recent studies on South Asian masculinities are often framed in terms of challenges and crises (Chakraborty 2017, Chopra, Osella & Osella 2004; Osella & Osella 2006; Dasgupta & Gokulsing 2014). Shifting gender relations, increasing female workforce and independence have left men confused about their role within family and society and, »this has led to confusion over the nature of masculine performance itself«, argue Dasgupta & Gokulsing (2014: 12f). This 'crisis' is a global one; nevertheless, it takes on a specific form in the Indian context, where it is shaped by the colonial encounter. Indian masculinities during the British era were created as a contrast to those of the colonizers, simultaneously as hypersexual and aggressive as well as effeminate and weak (ibid. 8). In response to colonial humiliation and following postcolonial confusion, literature presents Indian men as caught in a complex web of role models and social pressure.[6] These range from spiritual ideas of ascetism (paradigmatically represented by the figure of Gandhi), strong Hindu maleness, virile film heroes to global images of manhood and new conceptualizations like metrosexual masculinity, that link gendered performance and urbanity with media influence (Gehlawat 2012). Popular culture analysis offers further insights into the construction of changing male role models from the »Five-Year-Plan Hero« of the Nehruvian era to »angry young man« in the 1970s and 1980s (Srivastava 2014). Hindi cinema's dominating genre in the 1990s is the »domestic drama« or the »family film«, which usually features two main male characters, that of the immature young hero developing into a responsible and 'good' Indian man over the course of the narrative; and secondly, the benevolent patriarch (usually a father figure) who sanctions young people's relationships:

> The patriarchal agenda is furthered with misguided but benevolent fathers, reinforcing marriage as the foundational institution of society, maintaining traditional and

---

4   For example, Lapsansky & Chatterjee 2013; Mogford, Irby & Das 2015.
5   For example, Krishna Raj 2012; Bagchi 2017; Poggendorf-Kakar 2003.
6   See also Mangesh Kulkarni's body of works spanning over 20 years of research on historical and contemporary aspects of masculinity, i.e. »The Dark Subcontinent of Masculinity: Viewing Indian History through the Lens of Men's Studies« (2005).

sexist family values and abnegating individual identity for collectivity in favour of enlightened self-interest (Malhotra & Alagh 2004: 28).

As I will argue in this paper, similar forms of hegemonic patriarchy can be found in the contemporary attempts at reframing Indian fatherhood and they are inherently linked to the »crisis of masculinity«.

The academic void on Indian fatherhood is surprising in view of the government's current foregrounding of fathers' important role in bringing about progress and development. By targeting fathers, the BJP's family policy takes up the National Family Planning Program's trend. Since the 1990s, the Ministry of Health and Family Welfare (MoHFW) has intensified its efforts to combine family planning, in terms of fertility control, with other programs that are aimed at broader social change, such as an overall improvement of health and education, women's empowerment and poverty reduction (Chatterjee & Riley 2001: 826f). MoHFW changed »family planning« into »family welfare program« and now emphasises planned parenthood and a changed attitude towards age of marriage, dowry, son preference and female feticide. Chatterjee and Riley (2001: 811) argue, the Indian interventions in family planning are part of a broader postcolonial development agenda and represent both appropriation and resistance to hegemonic 'western' concepts of modernity. Within the national program of population control, the authors observe a selective indigenisation of 'modern' values. Terming it »engaged difference« (ibid. 818), they interpret the strategy in terms of domestication of a hegemonic concept of modernity.

The *Family Planning Program* can thus be understood as a profound intervention into a national future. In analogy to *#SelfieWithDaughter*, the MoHFW's multimedia campaigns propagate not only the two-child-norm (with son and daughter) but even the one-child-family, usually illustrated with a girl-child (ibid. 827). The rewards for responsible family planning in the Ministry's promotional campaigns is always depicted in material form. The didactic stories of well-planned, small and educated families emphasise their consumer power in many ways. The promised materialism has a recognizable Indian, local, and aspirational middle class character (ibid. 831). Fernandes (2000: 623) even states, the four members of the family ideal propagated by the state have given way to the image of the mobile modern nuclear family, consisting of father, mother, child and car. The most recent re-orientation of the Ministry's media campaigns since 2017 targets predominantly men as responsible for family planning and therewith deviates from the decades of women-centric campaigns (MoHFW Annual Report 2017-18: 92-96). The Family Planning Program's website *Hum Do* (We Two) explains »India's Strategy« in four principles:

1. Increased focus on spacing services without disturbing the sterilization pie.
2. Voluntary adoption of family planning based on felt need of the community.
3. Focus on male participation
4. Rights' based approach to family planning

(*Hum Do*, https://humdo.nhp.gov.in/about/national-fp-programme/, accessed September 18, 2019)

The Ministry of Health and Family Welfare 2017 multimedia campaign

In 2017, the Ministry launched a two-phase »360 degree multimedia campaign«, including film, print and outdoor advertising, which was initially promoted by famous actor Amitabh Bacchan (MoHFW Annual Report 2016-17: 94). The second phase of the campaign was launched in July 2017 at the celebration of the World Population Day. The Report states, the campaign was designed with the objective to »reaching out to people of all age groups, regions and strata of the society to bring about a positive change in the use of contraception and shatter the myths around it« (MoHFW Annual Report 2017-18: 93). The second phase involved the inception of the website *Hum Do* and a dedicated call center, four television commercials, a series of posters and hoardings, video messages circulated via WhatsApp and a weekly Sunday morning Radio Chat Show equally called »Hum Do« (MoHFW Annual Report 2017-18: 93-96). The messages portrayed across all media formats focused on new contraceptive methods, the involvement of men and the extended family in family planning, spacing between children and ideal timing for the first pregnancy after marriage. Overall, the health program advises newly married couples to wait two years after marriage to have their first child and then plan a gap of three years between consecutive children.

The series of short films and television commercials is probably the component with the widest reach and highest reception. The television commercials were broadcasted on national television and in audio formats on All India Radio. The television commercials can be found on the website *Hum Do* as well.[7] I assume the other promotional clips found on *Hum Do* are the ones that were circulated via WhatsApp and probably other social media,

---

7   I was unable to identify the agency, which the Ministry commissioned to develop the promotional films and television commercials.

but I was unable to verify this assumption. Two out of four television commercials feature husbands as lead characters and the spots' titles do not conceal the Ministry's approach. In »Mardangi« (»Manhood«)[8], viewers meet an excited but enlightened newly wedded husband, whereas in »Role of Men« a slightly older tractor-driving (married) man discusses family planning with his friends on a ride through the village. »Mardangi« is remarkable because it corresponds exactly to the state program's vision to create a new image of Indian manhood:

> Responsibility of men in family planning is the true sign of masculinity and the importance of promoting male engagement in family planning (MoHFW Annual Report 2017-18: 93).

The young groom is shown stealing away during his wedding celebration, to chat with three male friends in a parking bus. As already indicated by the spot's title, his friends tease him by asking, »What will real manhood be?« (kya hoge asli mardangi?). They hint at the sexual activities and quick production of children that are to follow the couple's wedding night. The jovial, masculine joking turns to a more pensive note, when the groom responds,

> Look, together with love one has to build responsibility. This is what real manhood consists of, no? (Dekhiye, pyaar ke saath zimmedaari bhi bana. Isi mein asli mardangi, hai na?) (Mardangi, 2017).[9]

The conversation circles around manhood, not fatherhood, and is for the three friends intrinsically linked to sexual activity and procreation, which reflects hegemonic ideas of manhood, virility and patriarchy. The style of conversation, use of words, and joking expressions of the men very authentically mirror a kind of coy but notorious engagement with topics of sexuality and the many taboos surrounding it, particularly observable among young men (see Strulik in this volume). The 'mature' comment of the groom does not negate these ideas and experiences but attempts at reframing the very idea of manhood, as understood within the heteronormative framework of marriage, by linking it with the concept of responsibility.

The commercial ends with a voiceover directed at young couples, which is identical in all four commercials.

> India is growing its family by being prepared from both health and thought. India is making its future firm. Call and get all information related to family planning. A

---

8   The TVCs and promotional material are accessible via https://humdo.
     nhp.gov.in/iec-material/video-materials/ (last accessed September 19, 2019).

9   National Health Portal, India. »Family Planning Mardangi 60sec«. July 20,
     2017.   https://www.youtube.com/watch?v=YyKtjdXq9BY&feature=
     youtu.be (last accessed 30.10.2019).

couple who plans its family is responsible. (Sehat aur soch donon se taiyaar hokar parivaar badha raha hai indiya. Apna bhavishya pakka bana raha hai indiya. Fon karen aur parivaar niyojan se judee sab jaanakaaree paie. Jodee zimmedaar jo plain kare parivaar.) (Mardangi, 2017).[10]

Again, the emphasis lies on responsibility, on planning, and on mutual decision-making by the couple. The rhetoric is notably patriotic in emphasizing India as active agent in the family planning process.

The second commercial, titled »Role of Men« (2017)[11], particularly attempts to remove the taboo associated with talking about reproductive health and contraception. The three men drive on a tractor through a village, talking about the wedding preparations for one of them. The driver does not say a word until they pass by a Family Planning Center, which he recommends to the groom-to-be. The other two men appear embarrassed and poke fun at him but he insists, that it is important to get an understanding for life after the wedding[12] (i.e. married life and family planning).

The promotional clip[13] »Mehnat« (»Hard work«) features several fathers promoting the recommended three-year-gap between children in order to keep the family happy and healthy. Another six videos feature amiable couples taking consensual decisions on contraception and birth spacing. All videos are located in a rural, lower class, and traditionally stylized setting. We often see children studying or playing in the background. This form of developmental discourse directly connects to the construction on an ideal family, but also to recent government programs such as *Beti Bachao Beti Padhao* (BBBP) or the images of loving and supportive parents taking selfies with their daughters.

Apart from the emphasis on men as key figures driving social 'progress', the campaign contains a remarkable commercial titled »Daadi« (Grandmother).[14] The Annual Report describes the objective as follows,

> Dispelling old notions and aims to mitigate the social pressures faced by newlyweds from elders and family members on bearing children immediately after marriage. (MoHFW Annual Report 2017-18: 94).

---

10   I thank Adele Hennig-Tembe for helping with the nuances of translation.
11   National Health Portal, India. »Family Planning« (R.O.M. 60sec). July 20, 2017. https://www.youtube.com/watch?v=sreMylrhrY8&feature=youtu. be (accessed 30.10.2019).
12   »Shaadi ke baad ke samajhdari taiyari karo!« (Role of Men, 2017).
13   The promotional clips did not air on television according to my knowledge.
14   National Health Portal, India. »Family Planning Dadi 60sec«. July 20, 2017. https://www.youtube.com/watch?v=8tCCXtNM_Uc&feature=youtu.be (last accessed 30.10.2019).

The commercial features a newlywed couple seeking the husband's grand-mother's blessings, upon which Daadi gives him a brochure on contraceptive methods to read. When he is visibly embarrassed, Daadi asks the shy young wife, who has not uttered a word so far, to continue. The grand-mother's 'modern' outlook creates a complicity between the two women and the narrative resolves into a relaxed atmosphere and ends with the voiceover mentioned above. Among the material of the 2017 multimedia campaign, »Daadi« is the only promotional video that takes up the extended family as important actors within the project of progress and development. The campaign thus recognizes the pressure issued by authorities within the family and pays credit to a lived reality, which seldom consists of an independent, well-informed couple that is in complete control over their family-related decisions. Within this clip, manhood takes a backseat and it is intergenerational female complicity (paired with rationality) that facilitates a changed outlook. As noted above, planning and modernity form a synthesis, which is made clear through the title of the brochure given to the couple: »Family planning methods have become modern« (aadhunik ho chuke hain parivaar niyojan ke tareeke) (Daadi, 2017).

Among these state-sponsored and state-supported endeavours to promote men as responsible husbands and fathers, #SelfieWithDaughter yields the highest visibility in national and international media discourses. This can partly be explained by its multimedia marketing strategy but has to be attributed also to Modi's endorsement. While the discussion in Indian news and social media ranges from affirmative to controversial, academic scholarship has merely mentioned the phenomenon as marginalia.

Men in Crises and Selfies with Daughters

On June 9, 2015 #SelfieWithDaughter started as a grassroots campaign, initiated by Sunil Jaglan, the *sarpanch*[15] of Bibipur village in the state of Haryana. The North Indian state is notorious for its patriarchal structures that facilitate an exclusion of women from most domains in the public sphere, a neglect of girl children and a disastrous sex ratio resulting of rampant female sex selective abortions and still present cases of female infanticide

---

15   A *sarpanch* (Hindi) is the elected head of the village-level constitutional body of local self-government called *(khap) panchayat*.

(Kaur 2010: 14).[16] One long-term effect is a shortage of women, particularly in the cohorts of marriageable age over the last 20 years. Prem Chowdhry (2005) argues that the current situation strongly affects the complexity of masculinities in present Haryana with increasing numbers of unmarried, unemployed and elderly men. She situates this »crisis of masculinity« (Chowdhry 2005) within the context of new technologies, globalization and consumerism and contends that this combination leads to greater aggression and violence, worsening gender equations and hence consolidates repressive social forces.

> These unemployed, unmarried males seek to gain status and power by asserting their power and masculinity by controlling 'errant' others. Whether it is caste revenge on a dalit or a khap panchayat[17] asserting itself in the matter of marriage, Haryanvi society points to tensions arising from an anomic state of society, in which other north Indian states are not far behind (Kaur 2010: 16).

To face the situation of the many 'surplus' Haryanvi men, a year before initiating #SelfieWithDaughter, Jaglan in his position as *sarpanch* set up an *Avivahit Purush Sangthan* (Unmarried Men's Association) in his village Bibipur (Kaur 2014: 18). In the run up to the 2014 elections, the Association had only one demand: »Bahu dilao, vote pao« (Get us a bride for our vote) (The Economic Times 2014). The particular context of Haryana is of utmost importance to the analysis of an endeavor like #SelfieWithDaughter, which strikes at the heart of the problem: The »crisis of masculinity«. The crisis may be eased by efforts towards an improved sex ratio, as is the stated goal of Jaglan, and it goes hand in hand with reframing manhood in terms of pro-daughter fatherhood. This indicates - irrespective of the campaign's name – that the daughter is not so much the central focus but the father, an argument I will extend later.

After his engagement with the 'male problem', Jaglan recalls his motivational experience for initiating #SelfieWithDaughter as framed by thoughts on »empowerment and emancipation of rural women«:

> When a nurse working with the hospital conveyed me about the birth of [my] girl child, simply treating the news a felicitation I handed over Rs. 2000 asking her to distribute sweets among all the staff members of hospital. But the response came to me as an utter surprise and shock both when the nurse refused to accept the money saying that it is done only at the birth of a boy child. This incident shook me to the core of my heart. Following that I managed to collect the data of child sex ratio of my village which was found to be dismally low. Having been engrossed with the

---

16   Haryana's current sex ratio stands at 877 women for 1,000 men. The child sex ratio is even worse with 830 girls for 1,000 boys (Kaur 2014: 18). See also John et. Al (2008) for further research on sex ratios in Northern India.

17   See footnote 12.

thought how to do for the empowerment and emancipation of rural women, I ,while watching a trailer of Salman Khan's film »*Bajrangi Bhai Jaan*«, was impressed with the lines of a song-»*Le Le Le Selfie Le*« since my daughter Nandini had picked my phone only to take her selfie [sic!] (http://selfiewithdaughter.world/about_in.aspx, last accessed September 20, 2019, emphasis in original).

It is remarkable how the narrative weaves together several discursive strands: Jaglan's personal disappointment at the hospital, his efforts to understand patriarchal structures at work on a micro-level the local social structures by learning about the situation of its immediate socio-geographical environment, the influence of popular media (a Hindi film song), and the ultimate link to contemporary technological innovation. Jaglan then spread the campaign on Facebook and WhatsApp to reach a wide audience and continuously conducted workshops and talks in educational institutions to promote his endeavour. The ultimate breakthrough came with Modi mentioning the campaign on June 28, 2015 during his monthly radio show »Mann Ki Baat«[18] which is broadcast on All India Radio as well as on national television (DD National, DD News). An app launch followed and the hashtag campaign received national and international recognition for raising awareness. In the context of populist media strategies Sinha writes, »#SelfieWithDaughter asked fathers to tweet photos with their daughters and created a ritual of union with the leader while reinforcing a patriarchal model of the family« (2017: 4170). Kaul (2017: 534) comments on Modi's promotion of the campaign as an attempt to stage himself as paternal figure, by which he tries to build on the politically significant »father figure« mythology.

Today, the Instagram hashtag #SelfieWithDaughter alone yields more than 5000 posts from all across the globe (September 17, 2019). The website hosts 90,800 uploaded selfies and claims 1,230,227 visitors. The »Latest Selfies« by default show 35 pictures, out of which 21 show fathers and daughter(s), 10 show mothers and daughters(s), and 4 show both parents and daughter(s).[19] With regard to the promotional strategy of the campaign, two arguments deserve closer attention. Firstly, Modi's endorsement creates a direct link to other pro-girl programs like *Beti Bachao Beti Padhao (BBBP)* with the ultimate goals to »enjoy the rising honour and prestige of our daughters« and to »rid ourselves of this bad name that we have for not respecting our daughters« (Modi quoted on http://selfiewithdaughter.world/, last accessed August 21, 2019). In this quote, the Prime Minister

---

18   »Mann Ki Baat« (Hindi) literally translates as »matters of the heart«.
19   The data was retrieved from http://selfiewithdaughter.world/Default.aspx, (last accessed August. 21, 2019).

does not mention an overall empowerment or challenge to patriarchal structures, but his main concern concentrates on »honour and prestige«, which corresponds to - as Hussain (2015) has called it with reference to Goffmann – an »'impression management' of India«.

The second interesting argument is part of the #SelfieWithDaughter Foundation's mission statement:

> We work to impart greater impetus to already laid government initiatives and campaigns for meeting the objective sensitisation of the society in general although *particularly of the males* towards the rights, equality, education, health, safety, participation and empowerment of girls and women. (http://selfiewithdaughter.world/about_Foundation.aspx, last accessed 21 August, 2019, emphasis by author).

Men as the target group reflect the disproportionate engagement of fathers with the campaign, although as the exemplary figures above show, mothers and parents in general feel addressed, too. »the overriding popularity of the campaign with fathers offers interesting insights into the location of fathers within the ideology of gender justice conceived by #SelfieWithDaughter campaign« (Hussain 2015). Following Hussain's suggestion, the next section explores the flip side of the campaign by looking at contested notions of gender justice and probes these arguments comparatively with the analytical insights from the Ministry of Health and Family Welfare (MoHFW) campaign.

Contested Notions of Gender Justice: #SelfieWithDaughter and 'real manhood'

Enthusiastic support was not the exclusive response to the campaign but critical voices came forward and created a heated online controversy rife with abuses. The online vitriol in defense of the campaign and the Prime Minister that followed critical comments made by Shruti Seth and Kavitha Krishnan drastically reveal the ineffectiveness of the campaign on a meta-level, which is in tackling ideologies of pervasive patriarchy and toxic masculinity, sexism, classism, and minority discrimination.

Actress Shruti Seth tweeted »Selfies don't bring about change, reform does. So please try and be bigger than a photograph. Come on!« and was subjected to 48 hours of non-stop nasty trolling in response (Seth 2015). Secretary of the All India Progressive Women's Association, activist and communist politician Kavitha Krishnan met a similar fate and reported later, »[t]he vitriol in defense of the prime minister was a cocktail of gross racism, homophobia, transphobia and graphic violence against women« (Krishnan 2015). Both, Seth and Krishnan, point out the highly ideological and simultaneously deeply gendered and abusive rhetoric directed against them. Their initial scepticism about the campaign is thereby strongly reinforced.

> What is the point of taking selfies with your girls when you're also responsible for creating the most toxic environment for them to grow up in? How will taking a photograph nullify the misogyny and patriarchy that is so deeply entrenched in our society? Why bother to increase the number of girls being born when you choose to treat them with such indignity and disrespect? (Seth 2015).

> My question is - how to go beyond superficial 'we respect women/protect daughters' posturing? After all, today's experience has proved that the same people tweeting #SelfieWithDaughter can also indulge easily in the most horrific verbal violence against women, and can advocate physical violence as a political tool. What's the point of posting selfies with daughters, if you can't oppose honour crimes against daughters? If you can't defend the freedom of every woman to express opinions in public space without being subjected to rape threats? (Krishnan 2015).

Above all, the campaign's desired effect is questionable, if the Prime Minister himself remains silent and continues following these abusive twitter handles, concludes Krishnan (2015).

Sociologist Saba M. Hussain goes beyond the analysis of immediate reactions and examines the campaign itself with regard to its proclaimed goal of strengthening gender justice. She stresses that the behaviour towards Seth and Krishnan indicates a lack of tolerance towards dissent but also reinforces a hierarchical distinction between protectable and 'bad' women who deserve violence and abuse.

Additionally, the very pre-conditions of the campaign that require the possession of a smart phone, internet access and »social acceptability of public expression of intimate emotions« (Hussain 2015) deepen a divide between (middle class) daughters that are worth saving and 'Others'. Certain backgrounds, such as parks, cars, malls, or a vacational mode, indicate the middle-classness of many posts. This represents a decisive departure from the imagery of the MoHFW television commercials, which are set in lower class, rural and rather traditional settings. While both initiatives target fathers/husbands, the underlying intention differs. They promote family planning in the sense of contraception, birth spacing, and general reproductive knowledge with the ultimate goals to increase the health and wellbeing of all family members and to decrease the Indian population. The short films directly address men as important decision-makers within the family by highlighting the connection between 'real manhood', responsibility and modernity. At the same time, mutual decision-making and a substantial unity of the couple is an integral part of the rhetoric. Planning and understanding serve as indicators of modernity, while 'real manhood' is the incentive for behavioural change, which nevertheless remains within a patriarchal framing by presenting men as decision-makers or by maintaining the authority of elders in portraying them giving 'modern' advice. Both strategies are partly continuation, partly reinvention of existing government technologies. State sponsored initiatives have never challenged the social structure per se. They have always promoted partial change in terms of development and modernisation. Within this ideological framework, the way in which men are addressed nevertheless represents a narrative shift in the continuous fabrication of an Indian modernity.

The fathers in #SelfieWithDaughter fulfil a different function than those in the Ministry's television commercials. They neither convey medicinal or educational messages, nor do they promote coupledom and decision-making at eye level, they simply pose with their daughters and thereby hint at embracing the idea that girls are as good as boys and that they are loving and proud fathers.

By painting over class distinctions and 'real' problems, the supporters of the selfie campaign are concealing forms of gendered violence, in particular against 'Other' (lower class, lower caste, non-Hindu) women, by focusing on the individual level of father-daughter relationships which is not necessarily connected to a meta-level of gender justice, as Jaglan's testimony of motivation attests. Hussain therefore claims the principle of gender justice as the biggest casualty of #SelfieWithDaughter: »People located across various ideological positions can now claim to be gender justice crusaders – without actually having to alter anything in their own lives and ideological make ups.« (Hussain 2015). Hussain's critique is similar to arguments made by Morozov (2013) and Gladwell (2010), who believe that cyberactivism does not translate into real movements. With little effort, it simply pacifies the social consciousness, hence the term »slacktivism« for low-risk activism by clicking »like«, signing petitions and forwarding pictures and articles emerged (Joseph 2012: 150).

In summing up her sociological insights from the campaign, Hussain points out three strategies that reinforce patriarchal gender hierarchies rather than combatting them. Very much in line with the current *Family Planning Program*, the campaign creates a figure, which she calls »the father-activist« whose personhood is hyper-visible and overshadows in most posts the individual personhood of the girls. Her invisibility is in many cases consistent with »the patriarchal framing of the father-daughter bond« (Hussain 2015). He is an activist simply by virtue of being a father and taking a selfie with his daughter, irrespective of his ideological leaning or opinion about greater social structures. Even patriarchal politicians pose with their daughters and chant along with the government's slogan »Beti bachao, beti padhao« in order to »save« and »protect« the daughters of the nation. By reinforcing the role of fathers in terms of protectionism, the campaign connects to a gendered discourse of safety, surveillance and restriction (Phadke 2007: 1511f). In this regard, the campaign again remarkably differs from the MoHFW approach, which also portrays men as 'activists' but equipped with a clear agenda.

The third argument that Hussain proposes is concerned with notions of pride in relation to the visualised father-daughter relationship. Sociologically, the idea of pride conveys similar emotions as honour, which are not »necessarily connected to achievements but pride is constituted in the subjectivity of the daughter i.e. 'pride' rests on conduct as a daughter« (Hussain 2015). Modi himself speaks of enjoying the »rising honour and prestige of our daughters«, which implicates a certain conduct or reputation of these honourable daughters. This discourse of pride also carries with it demands of surveillance in order to maintain or restore pride and honour. Interestingly, #SelfieWithDaughter features an exception to the above made claim on the invisibility of the girl's personhood by highlighting »Popular Faces« and »Inspiring Daughters«. »Popular Faces« (Image 1) foregrounds girls' extraordinary achievements, such as being the »Bronze Medalist Rio Olympics 2016", »Youngest Gold medalist in shooting in 2018 Commonwealth Games« or »Miss India 2017« (not in the picture).

Image 1 »Popular Faces«, http://selfiewithdaughter.world, last accessed September 24, 2019.

The »Popular Faces« are apparently the medalled daughters, but the father's name provides the caption nevertheless, the daughter is listed below. Even though the daughter appears as an individual, the framing remains within the patriarchal father-daughter imagery that conveys pride and protection-ism. This observation resembles the patriarchal framing of Hindi cinema's 1990s domestic dramas, in which the young protagonist always require blessings from the patriarchal authority in order to conclude with a happy end. »Popular faces« also directly connect to competitive sports and thereby refer to the great successes achieved by women, which represent India's ambition as emerging sports nation. The popularity of Indian sport dramas focussing on female athletes like »Chak De! India« (2007)[20] or »Mary Kom« (2014)[21], in a way anticipated the strategy of #SelfieWithDaughter by promoting a nexus of family and national pride that is based on women's success.[22] Nevertheless, despite adopting different representational and rhetorical strategies, the MoHFW television commercials as well as #SelfieWithDaughter create at first sight very positive and likeable images of Indian manhood.

Conclusion

The *#SelfieWithDaughter* campaign proves successful in reaching a wide, national and even global, audience, in inspiring participation and generating a media discourse on gender justice, the situation of girls and women in India, and India's Prime Minister Narendra Modi. It does so by emphasising individual father-daughter bonds of technology savvy middle class people. The campaign blends seamlessly with prior and following endeavours to target fathers as crucial agents of social change in the Family Planning Pro-gram's agenda, exemplified by MoHFW television commercials. While the projected ideals of the MoHFW campaign are embedded in narratives of health, rationality and a national vision of modernity, #SelfieWithDaughter remains comparatively vague in its ideological message. Despite the 'aware-ness' effect of the project, it remains limited to individual experience and does not transcend micro-level social structures to challenge ideologies of pervasive patriarchy, sexism, classism, and minority discrimination. No le-gal moves followed from the government. The overt emphasis on father and daughter as a 'team' is remarkable but does not withstand sociologically

---

20   The movie's narrative revolves around a Muslim coach who trains the Indian women's national hockey team to prove his loyalty to the nation.
21   A biographical film about the internationally successful female boxing star Mary Kom.
22   I thank Nadja-Christina Schneider for pointing out the connection between sport films, nationalism and the imagery of successful Indian daughters.

based feminist scrutiny, as Hussain's (2015) critical assessment of »armchair 'Father-activists' with dubious commitments to gender justice« demonstrates. If #SelfieWithDaughter neither facilitates gender justice, nor effects a substantial change in parenting, but rather reinforces patriarchal images of family life, what does the campaign actually tell us about contemporary gender and family politics?

This brings us back to the initial observation of a fundamental contradiction between the ruling BJP's conservative gender ideology and its concessions to gender mainstreaming by promoting schemes like BBBP. This paper concludes by offering three intertwining interpretations in response to the question about the intentions a Hindu right-wing government might have in promoting a campaign like #SelfieWithDaughter.

First, an appropriation of hegemonic discourses of modernity, that is inclusive and gender-just, might be strategically useful in order to secure India's position as globally powerful player. »The campaign is enabling certain sections of Indian society to create a temporary but widely circulated social image of themselves that aligns with the Indian's aspirational economic image of a neoliberal powerhouse« (Hussain 2015). The aspirational aspect of global modernity resonates with Chatterjee and Riley's observation,

> Reason and agency, planning, male familial responsibility, female literacy, higher age at marriage, an absence of son preference, and perception of children as costs or investments are all presented as aspects of a total package of modernity that is directly indexed through material prosperity (Chatterjee & Riley 2001: 835).

Adding to the »total package of modernity«, »[a]n educated daughter is also a sign of enlightenment and investment« (ibid. 813f).

Second, the increased focus on men as agents of social change aims at establishing a more positive and gender-sensitive image of Indian men against the backdrop of a »crisis of masculinity« and a growing global awareness of patriarchy and male sexism in the wake of #metoo. On a national level, this might be a response to the discourse of 'rape culture' and the 'demonization' of Indian men in the aftermath of the Delhi gang rape case (Schneider & Titzmann 2014).

Third, gender mainstreaming initiatives can be seen as a strategic concession to India's female population. Women make up 50% of the population and constitute a lucrative vote bank. In the run up to the 2019 Lok Sabha elections, the campaigns of all parties laid emphasis on so-called »women-centric« themes (Thekaekara 2019). These were the first national elections where the women voters equalled that of men. Although women obtained the right to vote with India's independence in 1947, their voting behaviour was for a long time considered merely an expansion of their husband's voting decision (Kamra 2019). By addressing girls (indirectly as future voters) in a benevolent way, the Prime Minister and his government create a positive and accessible image of themselves.[23]

Addressing fathers and husbands, therefore, does promote responsible manhood and fatherhood but precisely within a hegemonic framework, that advocates fathers as patriarchal protectors. *Hum Do* enhances responsible parenthood by emphasising the couple as decision-makers and portraying rational men who have their family's welfare in mind. In conclusion, this tells us a lot about the persistent hegemonic patriarchy in contemporary Indian society but it also indicates an increasing pressure for change, which the women's movement, the Left, global media, as well as billions of Indian women exert. All three suggested approaches intertwine in a way that they aim at producing a certain image of Indian society, represented through 'progressive' steps taken by the Modi government. The discursive struggle over the meaning of gender equality takes a central position within the struggle over a national image and identity. Equality means many things to many people. Following Kapur and Cossmann (1993), who look at religion and gender equality as contradictory but mutually constituting concepts, the BJP's gender mainstreaming policy represents a tactical discursive move. It secures the government's legitimation, while simultaneously establishing their particular variation of patriarchal gender mainstreaming policy as hegemonic.

References

Bagchi, Jasodhara (2017): *Interrogating Motherhood.* Thousand Oaks: Sage.

Chakraborty, Chandrima (2017*). Mapping South Asian Masculinities: Men and Political Crises.* New York: Routledge.

Chatterjee, Nilanjana; Riley, Nancy E. (2001): »Planning an Indian Modernity: The Gendered Politics of Fertility Control«. *Signs: Journal of Women in Culture and Society* 26(3): 811-845.

---

[23] A shift towards women as national heroines is observable on several levels. The 2015 Republic Day Parade featured for the first time in history an all-women army contingent and in 2019 again TV anchors proudly presented India's »nari shakti« (women power) during the event (India Today 2019).

Chopra, Radhika; Caroline Osella, and Osella, Filippo (2004). *South Asian Masculinities: Context of Change, Sites of Continuity.* New Delhi: Women Unlimited an Associate of Kali for Women.

Chowdhry, Prem (2005). »Crisis of Masculinity in Haryana«. *Economic and Political Weekly* 40(49): 5189-5198.

Dadi (2017). National Health Portal, India. »Family Planning Dadi 60sec«. July 20, 2017. https://www.youtube.com/watch?v=8tCCXtNM_Uc&feature=youtu.be (last accessed 30.10.2019).

Dasgupta, Rohit K. and Gokulsing, Moti (2014). *Masculinity and its Challenges in India: Essays on Changing Perceptions.* Jefferson, NC: McFarland.

Fernandes, Leela (2000). »Nationalizing 'the Global': Media Images, Cultural Politics and the Middle Class in India«. *Media, Culture & Society* 22(5):611–628.

Gehlawat, Ajay (2012): »'Aadat Se Majboor'/'Helpless by Habit': Metrosexual Masculinity in Contemporary Bollywood«. *Studies in South Asian Film & Media* 4(1): 61–79.

Gladwell, Malcolm (2010). »Small Change. Why the Revolution Will Not Be Tweeted«. *The New Yorker*, October 04, 2010.

Goffmann, Erving (1956): *The Presentation of Self in Everyday Life.* Edinburgh: University of Edinburgh, Social Sciences Research Centre.

Hussain, Saba M. (2015). »The Sociology of #SelfieWithDaughter«, kafila.org, 09.07.2015. https://kafila.online/2015/07/09/the-sociology-ofselfiewithdaughter-saba-m-hussain/(last accessed September 23, 2019).

India Today, »WATCH: Nari Shakti on Full Display at Republic Day Parade«, January 26, 2019. https://www.indiatoday.in/india/video/watch-nari-shakti-on-full-display-at-republic-day-parade-1439942-2019-01-26 (last accessed November 11, 2019).

John, Mary E.; Kaur, Ravinder; Palriwala, Rajni; Raju, Saraswati; Sagar, Alpana. (2008). *Planning Families, Planning Gender: Addressing the Adverse Sex Ratio in Selected Districts of Madhya Pradesh, Rajasthan, Himachal Pradesh, Haryana and Punjab, With Support from ActionAid India and IDRC.* Canada, Books for Change.

Joseph, Sarah (2012). »Social Media, Political Change, and Human Rights«. *Boston College International and Comparative Law Review* 35(1): 145–188.

Kamra, Lipika (2019). »Women Voters and the 2019 Indian Elections«. *Jindal School of Liberal Arts & Humanities: Asia Dialogue*, 27th March 2019: http://jslh.edu.in/women-voters-and-the-2019-indian-elections/ (last accessed September 25, 2019).

Kapur, Rathna; Cossmann, Brenda (1993). "Communilising Gender/Engendering Community: Women, Legal Discourse and Saffron Agenda." Economic and Political Weekly 28(1): WS35-WS44.

Kaur, Ravinder (2010). »Khap Panchayats, Sex Ratio and Female Agency«. *Economic and Political Weekly* 45(23): 14-16.

Kaur, Ravinder (2014). »Sex Ratio, Khaps and Marriage Reform«. *Economic and Political Weekly* 49(31): 18-20.

Krishna Raj, Maithreyi (2012). *Motherhood in India: Glorification Without Empowerment?* London: Routledge.

Krishnan, Kavitha (2015). »Kavita Krishnan on Why #SelfieWithDaughter Proves Hollow. What Really Is the Point If You Find It Acceptable to Shower Sexist Abuse on Women Whom You Disagree With?« *dailyO*, 30.06.2015. https://www.dailyo.in/politics/selfie-with-daughter-modi-mann-ki-baat-kavita-krishnan-twitter-aloknath/story/1/4669.html (last accessed September 23, 2019).

Kulkarni, Mangesh (2005). »The Dark Subcontinent of Masculinity: Viewing Indian History Through the Lens of Men's Studies« In: K. K. Shah (Ed.) *History and Gender*. Rawat: Jaipur.

Lapsansky, Charlotte; Chatterjee, Joyee S. (2013). »Masculinity Matters: Using Entertainment Education to Engage Men in Ending Violence Against Women in India«. *Critical Arts* 27(1): 36-55.

Malhotra, Sheena; Alagh, Tavishi (2004). »Dreaming the Nation. Domestic Dramas in Hindi Films Post-1990«. *South Asian Popular Culture* 2(1): 19–37.

Mardangi (2017). National Health Portal, India. »Family Planning Mardangi 60sec«. July 20, 2017. https://www.youtube.com/watch?v=YyKtjdXq9BY&feature=youtu.be (last accessed 30.10.2019).

Mines, Diane P.; Lamb, Sarah (2002). *Everyday Life in South Asia*. Bloomington: Indiana University Press.

Ministry of Health & Family Welfare (MoHFW). Government of India. »Hum Do«. https://humdo.nhp.gov.in/iec-material/video-materials/ (alast ccessed September 19, 2019).

Ministry of Health and Family Welfare (MoHFW). Government of India. *Annual Report 2016-17, Chapter 6: Family Planning*, pp. 81-99. https://mohfw.gov.in/annual-report-department-health-and-family-welfare--2016-17 (last accessed August 16, 2019).

Ministry of Health and Family Welfare (MoHFW). Government of India. *Annual Report 2017-18, Chapter 6: Family Planning*, pp. 85-108. https://mohfw.gov.in/sites/default/files/06Chapter.pdf (last accessed August 16, 2019).

Mogford, Elizabeth; Irby, Courtney; Das, Abhijit (2015). »Changing Men to Change Gender: Combatting Hegemonic Masculinity Through Antiviolence Activism in Northern India«. *International Journal of Sociology of the Family*. 41(2): 71-93.

Morozov, Evgeny. *To Save Everything, Click Here: The Folly of Technological Solutionism*. New York: Public Affairs, 2013.

Osella, Caroline; Osella, Filippo (2006). *Men and Masculinities in South India*. London: Anthem Press.

Pernau, Margrit; Imtiaz, Ahmad; Reifeld, Helmut (2003). *Family and Gender: Changing Values in Germany and India*. New Delhi: Sage Publications.

Phadke, Shilpa (2007): »Dangerous Liaisons. Women and Men: Risk and Reputation in Mumbai«. *Economic and Political Weekly* 42(17): 1510–1518.

Poggendorf-Kakar, Katharina (2003). »Virtuous Mother, Virile Hero and Warrior Queen: The Conception of Gender and Family in Hindutva«. In: Pernau, M., Ahmad,

I., H. Reifeld, H. (Eds.). *Family and Gender: Changing Values in Germany and India.* New Delhi: Sage Publications. 179-195.

Role of Men (2017). National Health Portal, India. »Family Planning« (R.O.M. 60sec). July 20, 2017. https://www.youtube.com/watch?v=sreMylrhrY8&feature=youtu.be (last accessed 30.10.2019).

Saraff, Anjula; Srivastava, Harish C. (2008). »Envisioning Fatherhood: Indian Fathers' Perceptions of an Ideal Father Authors«. *Population Review* 47(1): 45-59.

Schneider, Nadja-Christina; Titzmann, Fritzi-Marie (Eds.) (2014): *Studying Youth, Media and Gender in Post-Liberalisation India Focus on and Beyond the 'Delhi Gang Rape'.* Berlin: Frank & Timme.

Selfie With Daughter by Sunil Jaglan. http://selfiewithdaughter.world/ (last accessed August 19, 2019).

Seth, Shruti (2015). @SethShruti, A Little Note to India. TwitLonger, 02.07.2015. http://www.twitlonger.com/show/n_1smtdi6 (last accessed September 25, 2019).

Sriram, Rajalakshmi (2019): *Fathering in India. Images and Realities.* Singapore: Springer.

Sriram, Rajalakshmi (2011): »Evidence of Change and Continuity in Fathering: The Case of Western India«. *Marriage & Family Review* 47(8): 625-647,

Srivastava, Sanjay (2014). »'Sane Sex.' The Five-Year Plan Hero and Men on Footpaths and in Gated Communities: On the Cultures of Twentieth-Century Masculinity«. In: Dasgupta, Rohit K. and Gokulsing, Moti (Eds.). *Masculinity and Its challenges in India: Essays on Changing Perceptions.* Jefferson, NC: McFarland. 27-53.

Tasveer Ghar. *Manly Matters.* http://www.tasveergharindia.net/essay/manly-matters-vision-statement.html (last accessed September 18, 2019).

The Economic Times (2014): »'Get Us Brides in Return for Our Votes': Haryana Bachelors to Candidates«, April 9, https://economictimes.indiatimes.com/news/politics-and-nation/get-us-brides-in-return-for-our-votes-haryana-bachelors-to-candidates/articleshow/33493084.cms (last accessed November 4, 2019).

Thekaekara, Mari Marcel (2019). »Have India's Women Seized Their Chance to Vote for a Safer, More Equal Country?« *The Guardian*, 20.05.2019. https://www.theguardian.com/commentisfree/2019/may/20/india-women-vote-safer-equal-bjp-election (accessed September 25, 2019).

Chapter 2: Present Absence of the »Other Mother«: Documentary Images and the Communicative Figuration Surrounding Gestational Surrogacy[24]

Nadja-Christina Schneider

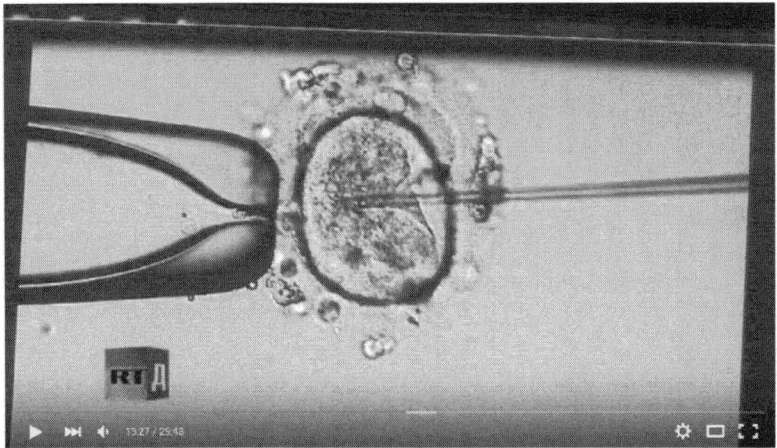

Image 1: From »traditional surrogacy« to »gestational surrogacy«: Visualization of Intracytoplasmic Sperm Injection Procedure (ICSI) (Source of Image: »Wombs for Rent in India« - produced for *Russia Today*, 2015). Number of clicks/views of this TV documentary on YouTube in August 2019: more than 1.9 million; number of comments on YouTube: more than 1.390.

As anthropologist Marilyn Strathern argues in her article »Still Giving Nature a Helping Hand? Surrogacy: a Debate About Technology and Society«, the interlocking of technological innovations and societal changes is a question our attention is usually only drawn to after this interrelationship has been made visible by the media or other »channels of mediation« (Strathern, 2002: 985). Which means that at the time of its becoming a public matter of comment and discussion, the actual innovation is already something which happened in the past and we as non-experts are literally not able to »see that prior process of change« independently (ibid.).

---

24   A longer version of this chapter has been published in *BioScope: South Asian Screen Studies* 2018 9(2): 184-207.

The biotechnological[25] innovation visualized in the still above definitely marked a watershed moment in the recent history of technologically assisted reproduction. The moment and procedure, which is made visible here in the *Russia Today* documentary »Wombs for rent in India« (2015), is called the intracytoplasmic sperm injection, or ICSI.

The transvaginal retrieval of oocytes allows for the direct injection of sperm into the ova and hence for a fertilization outside the body. This procedure has existed since 1992 and has since then become the standard procedure of technologically assisted reproduction, thereby developing further and increasingly replacing the conventional in vitro fertilization in which the egg and sperm are manually combined in a laboratory dish. As a result of this repro-technological innovation, up to five persons can now be involved in the process of creating a new baby. The procedure can be done using the so-called intended mother's own egg cells and her partner's sperm. Or it may involve eggs, sperm or embryos from a known or anonymous donor. Moreover, in many cases, a surrogate mother or so-called »gestational carrier« is used, who has an embryo implanted in her uterus. As a consequence, the presence and increasingly important role of the sperm donor, surrogate mother - and since the 1990s also the third figure of the egg donor - for the social reproduction of biological and genetically related families all over the world are now hard to ignore. While the altruistic language and terms such as »donors« and »surrogates« conceal the rapid worldwide commercialization of gametes, it is important to keep in mind that many different forms of non-commercial actual donations of sperms, eggs as well as gestation and delivery of a baby are currently also increasingly practiced in many parts of the world.[26] Besides the growing commercialization, another important aspect which is concealed by the altruistic language of »donation«, is the social inequality and hierarchy which has become a defining moment of technologically assisted reproduction since the beginning of the

---

25   There have been numerous attempts over the last decades or so to theorize the relationship between biotechnologies and their capitalization, notably by scholars working in the field of Science and Technology Studies. Theoretical approaches and concepts which have emerged from this academic field include, among others, *biovalue* (Waldby 2000), *bioeconomy* (Rose 2001), *biocapital* (Rajan 2006), and *life as surplus* (Cooper 2008). Even though Kaushik Sunder Rajan did not coin the term, his book »Biocapital: The Constitution of Postgenomic Life« (2006) has popularized it worldwide.

26   Aditya Bharadwaj mentions the various »altruistic« arrangements between family members in India who would »routinely seek out specific private clinics to help arrange a quick surrogate pregnancy«. He argues this »mode of, non-commercial family forming creates different but equally important sets of relations of exploitation, piety, kinship, and support« (Bharadwaj, 2012: 139f.).

era of commercial surrogacy in the late 1970s (Bernard, 2014: 278ff.). Over a period of two decades, the »surrogate mother« used to be a woman who agreed to carry her own genetic child for another couple.

Since the end of the 1990s, however, the new form of gestational surrogacy, in which the surrogate mother has no genetic relationship to the child that she agrees to carry and deliver for the intended parents, has become more and more prominent. As cultural historian Andreas Bernard argues,

---

The Surrogacy (Regulation) Bill, 2019

Salient features of the bill are:

- To allow *altruistic ethical* surrogacy to intending infertile couple between the age of 23-50 years and 26-55 years for female and male respectively.
- The intending couples should be legally married for at least five years and should be Indian citizens.
- The child born through surrogacy will have the same rights as are available for the biological child.
- The surrogate mother should be a *close relative* of the intending couple and should be between the age of 25-35 years. She can act as surrogate mother *only once.*
- The surrogate mother will carry a child which is *genetically related* to the Intending Couple.

Source: http://www.prsindia.org/billtrack/surrogacy-regulation-bill-2019 (last accessed: Aug 12, 2019)

---

the social inequality and hierarchy between commissioning parents and surrogate mothers increased significantly from the moment on when the surrogate was no longer necessarily genetically related to the baby, and the color of her skin was hence no longer of relevance to the intending parents (ibid.). Together with Thailand, India came to be known as one of the surrogacy hubs in Asia and for more than ten years, transnational surrogacy was a thriving business in this country. Despite the legal ban on commercial surrogacy in 2015, it has not been terminated completely according to press reports.[27] The assisted reproduction sector in India has been reported as being worth several hundred million dollars or even more than two billion

---

27   For instance, sociologist Sharmila Rudrappa describes in an interview with *U.S. News* how surrogate mothers from Kenya were now flown into Mumbai where the fertilized embryos were implanted into the uterus. After spending 24 weeks of their pregnancy in India, they were flown back to Nairobi to give birth to the baby in a designated clinic. According to Rudrappa, the doctor in charge in the Mumbai clinic maintained that »he had not broken the law, because technically,

dollars in recent years, depending upon the source. It is rather difficult to measure the commercial value of an industry that had been legal in India since 2002 but never regulated, in spite of repeated attempts to draft and pass a comprehensive ART legislation. A number of widely circulated and viewed documentary films, such as »Google Baby« (dir. Zippi Brand Frank, 2009), »Can we see the baby bump, please?« (dir. Surabhi Sharma, 2013) or »House of Surrogates« (dir. Matt Rudge, 2013), have functioned as a starting and major reference point for the debate about the complex issue of assisted reproductive medicine and transnational surrogacy in India. These films can also be said to have co-created »iconic« images and narratives which were subsequently taken up or developed further in various other formats and media, for instance in documentary theatre, journalistic report-ages, fictional films, or novels. Despite this observation, little attention has been paid to the remarkable intertextual and intermedial references which, as this chapter would like to show, have added significantly to the estab-lishment of a number of more or less »standardized« stories and visual rep-resentations in documentary mediations of the topic.[28] A contextualised analysis and comparison of documentary mediations can also shed light on the interconnectedness of different media formats and communicative prac-tices, and hence on their contribution to an emerging communicative fig-uration.[29] However, it should be mentioned that this applies primarily to

---

he had not interacted with gay clients within Indian territory, and all he had pro-vided was in vitro fertilization for Kenyan 'healthcare' seekers«. Sharmila Ru-drappa, »In India, Commercial Surrogacy Continues Despite Ban. Instead of Banning Commercial Surrogacy, Countries Should Regulate the Practice to Bet-ter Protect the Birth Mother from Exploitation«, *U.S. News*, Oct 26, 2017.

28   There are only a few academic articles or book chapters which refer to docu-mentaries on transnational surrogacy, such as Sayani Mitra and Solveig Lena Hansen's article »On the Other Side of the Camera. Surrogacy in India and the Moral Concern of the Film Maker Surabhi Sharma« [Auf der anderen Seite der Kamera. Leihmutterschaft in Indien und das moralische Anliegen der Dokumen-tarfilmerin Surabhi Sharma] which includes an interview with the director Surabhi Sharma. Published in German in: *Ethik in der Medizin* 27.1 (2015): 69-80; and Karen Hvidtfeldt Madsen (2015). »Documentaries on Transnational Surrogacy in India: Questions of Privilege, Respectability and Kinship«. In Krøløkke, Charlotte; Myong, Lene et al. (eds.). *Critical Kinship Studies*. Row-man & Littlefield International. 117-132. And Samel Yancey Sessions (2012). »Made in India. A Film About Surrogacy«. *Journal of the American Medical Association* 308(8): 818-819.

29   Andreas Hepp and the communicative figurations research network at the Uni-versity of Bremen suggest the model of communicative figurations which form around certain themes and which are generated by a multitude of different me-dia, actors and communicative practices.

transnational communicative spaces and contexts in which commissioning parents from the so-called global North are involved (who may sometimes also happen to be of Indian origin). In contrast, to understand how the procedures and societal repercussions of assisted reproductive technologies are mediated to audiences in India, the focus would have to be laid first of all on a number of famous actors or directors and their important role in facilitating an understanding that surrogacy can be seen as a legitimate means of obtaining a child. Most notably, Aamir Khan - the so-called »poster boy« for the surrogacy industry in India (Majumdar, 2014a: 120) - and his wife Kiran Rao who were one of the first celebrity couples to declare that their son Azad was born through a surrogate mother (see for instance, »Surrogacy Was Our Last Resort«, *India Today*, July 22, 2013). Much more controversy surrounded the surrogacy which was commissioned by Shah Rukh Khan and his wife Gauri because of the alleged prenatal sex determination for their third child and second son, AbRam. Interestingly, the coverage and discussion was, once again, very different when actor Tusshar Kapoor became the single father of a son by an Indian surrogate in 2016 (and half a year later, film producer and director Karan Johar became a father of twins through surrogacy), as at least the English-language press reacted with enthusiastic approval lauding the actor's »bold step« and his »new age fatherhood« repeatedly. In particular since former minister of external affairs of India, Sushma Swaraj, sharply criticized members of the Hindi film industry for abusing the possibilities of surrogacy - and in the same breath declared that the new surrogacy bill would unequivocally bar couples in live-in relationships, as well as same-sex couples and single parents from accessing the prospectively solely legal form of, so-called altruistic, surrogacy - the question of who and what family is allowed to be in India has been discussed in a remarkably lively and public manner.[30] It might hence appear exceptionally ironic that ever since the proclamation of the ban on commercial surrogacy in India in October 2015, of all things, entirely new ways of thinking and living family and kinship have become as strongly visible in Indian media as hardly ever before. Nevertheless, what does not seem to have changed is the ongoing fundamental invisibility and erasure of the surrogates themselves, as sociologist Anindita Majumdar has called it in her analysis of the coverage on commercial surrogacy in Indian print media (Majumdar 2014a). And this »fazing her out of the narrative altogether«

---

30   See for instance (unknown author) »Supermom of State, Sushma Swaraj, Gifts India a Sanskari Surrogacy Bill. Only Married Indian Citizen Couples Can Opt for 'Altruistic Surrogacy', But Not Our Singles, LGBTQ or Those in Live-in Relationships«. *DailyO*, 24 Aug 2016.

(ibid.: 109) is reiterated every time a celebrity publicly and eloquently thanks the doctors at fertility clinics - or even »the universe«, as did Karan Johar on the occasion of his children's first birthday in February 2017- for their surrogacy-born children - but hardly ever bother to even mention the surrogate and her labor.

As sociologist Amrita Pande convincingly argues in her long-term ethnographic study of commercial surrogacy in India, specifically focusing on Nayana Patel's famous (and visually much overrepresented) fertility clinic in Anand in Gujarat, the clinic aims at producing so-called »perfect mother-workers«. Mother-workers or surrogates constantly have to manipulate and discipline their own emotions and affects, she argues, in order to care for the unborn child as if it was their own. At the same time, they are told repeatedly to think of the baby as the genetic child of others that does not belong to them and to keep the contractual relationship between them and the commissioning parents as well as the clinic constantly in mind. Furthermore, their sense of guilt and obligation towards their own children is also systematically deployed by the clinic as an additional disciplinary tool to shape and produce the targeted perfect mother-workers (Pande 2014). Transnational reproduction and especially the three hitherto peripheral figures of the biological family, i.e. the sperm donor, the egg cell donor or the surrogate mother, are certainly no longer under-researched or underrepresented topics in current academic as well as non-academic debates. Quite on the contrary, there is a growing number of excellent ethnographic studies and elaborate theoretical discussions as well as an abundance of fictional and non-fictional films, TV series, documentary theater productions or novels that all focus on the complex reconfigurations of family, kinship and parenthood in a global age of increasingly biotechnologized and medicalized bodies. However, precisely the aspect of labor is often neglected or even concealed in this context, especially with regard to surrogate workers. What we encounter instead is the much-overused metaphor of the »rented womb« or »womb for rent« in far too many titles and visualizations, as will be shown further below.

Documentary Films as »Channels of Mediation«

The body of documentaries on commercial surrogacy in India can be roughly divided into two categories, first of all the largest group of documentary films which were produced for trans/national television networks (mainly in the USA, Russia and Great Britain) and secondly, a much smaller and less easily accessible group of independently produced documentary films. The latter category can be further divided into a subgroup of films by directors who predominantly live and work in the so-called global North and those who live and work mostly in India. Examples for the first category would be the above-mentioned film »Wombs for Rent in India« by RT Documentary (26min, 2015); »House of Surrogates« by Matt Rudge (BBC 4)(90min, 2013); »Made in India« by Rebecca Haimowitz and Vaishali Sinha (PBS/USA)(95min, 2010) and »Google Baby« by Zippi Brand Frank (HBO/USA)(69min, 2009). Examples for the second category would be »Ma Na Sapna - A Mother's Dream« by Valerie Gudenus (86min, 2013); »Can We See the Baby Bump Please« by Surabhi Sharma (49min, 2013); »Womb on Rent« by Ishani Dutta (49min, 2013) and »Mother Anonymous« by Rahul Ranadive (as part of Sheela Saravana's research on surrogacy in Mumbai) (10min, 2011).

The documentaries that I will mainly focus on in this chapter belong mostly to the first category, as they were either commissioned by transnational television channels, by national commercial TV production companies or non-commercial services such as PBS. I consider these documentaries as the internationally most visible and widely circulated films and some of them are also quite often referred to in journalistic articles as well as in discussions in various other media. I would like to distinguish these films, which were all made by professional documentary filmmakers, from a much larger number of reportages that are also sometimes done in a documentary-style format but often involve much less context-related research and generally only very short stays in India. These reportages may also be watched and commented upon by large numbers of viewers on YouTube. But unlike the documentaries in focus here, they mostly do not seem to travel across the different societal domains of knowledge and debate that Strathern talks about in her above-quoted article and, accordingly, can only be partly considered as »channels of mediation« (Strathern, 2002).

Following James Bennett and Nikki Strange's elaborate discussion of »Television as Digital Media« (2011), documentary films can no longer be seen in isolation as they are increasingly embedded in a new, digital (and social) media context (ibid.: 1). They are hence not just »televisual or cinematic«, but take on a variety of forms as they move or are distributed across multiple platforms. However, it is important to bear in mind that older forms still co-exist with new forms and this also pertains to the pluralization of viewing practices, as every service or platform brings its own »viewing protocols to bear on the experience of content« (ibid., see also Sorensen 2013: 52).

I. Translocal Circuits and Connectivities of Technologically Assisted Reproduction: »Google Baby« (2009)

One of the internationally best-known documentaries about transnational surrogacy and reproductive tourism in India is »Google Baby«. The award-winning film, which was directed by Zippi Brand Frank, a former TV journalist from Israel, is exemplary in the way in which it visualizes and contextualizes all the new global connectivities, actors and technologies as well as the practices which together bring forth the transnational reproductive market. »Google Baby« is centered around Doron Mamet, the founder and CEO of Tammuz, a transnational agency catering to intended parents from Israel and providing them with egg cells from donors in the United States which are then fertilized and taken to India where they are implanted into the womb of a surrogate mother, somewhere »in the suburbs of Mumbai or Delhi« as it says on an older version of the website of the agency, or they are selected »from Tammuz's pool« and then »relocated with their families to accommodation provided in Kathmandu«. The film was produced by Sheila Nevins and Yona Wiesenthal and made its debut in Israel in 2009, it was later purchased by the US American cable network HBO. The film is also available on YouTube in several different versions and has been clicked or watched more than 100,000 times online. Many press reviews mention, with some amazement, the »striking neutrality« of the documentary which never seems to judge the practices that it illuminates or to take a definite stand against commercial surrogacy and split parenthood. The film's openness to diverse readings is also clearly confirmed by some of the highly contrasting comments posted by viewers on YouTube, ranging from pro-surrogacy statements and sympathetic remarks towards the commissioning parents to expressions of puzzlement or outright shock and disgust about the outsourcing pregnancies.[31] Likewise, comments on widely shared documentaries show that these films may not only serve as a starting point for critical debate and introspection, but sometimes also primarily as a source of information for potential intending parents, as one comment posted by »r person« (posted in 2013) indicates:

> My partner and I watched this documentary (i.e. «Google Baby») - and - decided to go this route. (…) We are due in April. THANK YOU for drawing so much attention to this. It's one thing to fly under the radar, it's another to become the gay

---

31   Comments and responses can be found at: https://www.youtube.com/
watch?v=pQGlAM0iWFM (last accessed Aug 14, 2019)

parent capitol of the world! Had things remained contained, I would not be panicking as to what I will do now that singles and gays are barred, care to donate some funds to help? (ibid.).

Director Zippi Brand Frank confirmed in press interviews that she does not condemn the practices of sperm, egg donation and commercial surrogacy entirely, but she clearly expressed hopes for her film to support demands for a regulation to avoid the exploitation or surrogate workers and babies as mere commodities.[32]

As mentioned above, even before the Indian government announced in October 2015 that it would ban foreigners from seeking surrogacy in India, non-heterosexual couples, non-married couples and singles had already been excluded from the group of foreign nationals that could apply for a »Medical Visa«. However, this was not the case in Nepal so that agencies like Tammuz could use the existing legal loopholes, hire a surrogate mother in India and »relocate« her across the border. This cross-border business became only visible in the Indian and international news media when Israel evacuated babies from Nepal after the earthquake in April 2015, while the surrogates who had carried and delivered these babies had been left behind and most of them were actually from India.[33] In the wake of the negative coverage and massive critique, the government in Nepal announced shortly afterwards that it would ban foreigners from seeking surrogacy in the country, as Thailand and India had already announced earlier in the same year.[34]

---

32   See for istance Abigail Klein Leichman (2011). »The Israeli Mom Behind Google Baby«. *Israel21*. Oct 27, 2011.

33   See for instance Aeyal Gross (2015). »It Takes an Earthquake in Nepal to Talk About Surrogacy in Israel.« *Haaretz*. April 30, 2015.
Alon-Lee Green (2015). »Where Is the Concern for the Surrogate Mothers in Nepal?« *Haaretz*. April 27, 2015.

34   Many experts in India, including women's rights and reproductive health advocacy organizations like SAMA, argued that the ban and criminalization of commercial surrogacy was not really about the protection of poor women but in fact made them even more vulnerable as the industry would simply go underground. In their view, the long-awaited strict regulation of the surrogacy market in India would thus have been better than the partial ban. Priyanka Vora (2017). »Surrogacy in India: Parliamentary Committee Reopens the Surrogacy Debate, Says Commercial Surrogacy Should Be Allowed.« *Scroll.in*. August 17, 2017.

II. Intermedial References and Intertextual Borrowings: »The House of Surrogates« (2013)

As indicated above, it is particularly interesting to observe that documentary films create images and tell stories which are often taken up and developed further in various other documentary or fictional formats. The novel titled »The House of Hidden Mothers« by British-Indian actress, comedian, screenwriter and novelist Meera Syal which was published in June 2015, shall serve to illustrate this observation. The novel was well received by critics and audiences, especially in the UK. Syal was also willing to play her role as an »insider« and »authentic expert« and spoke engagingly in television interviews about the perils of the surrogacy industry in India. This is of course a phenomenon which has been apparent particularly in the »packaging« and marketing of documentary and fictional films for quite some time now: In view of the competitive and profoundly changing nature of national and transnational television production, it is becoming crucial to raise interest in essential issues through credible testimonials, such as »authentic« actors or other »experts«, and to communicate relevant stories which inform and engage audiences in an equally entertaining and instructive manner (see also the following chapter in this book). Against this background, the question regarding the role of the production and knowledge transfer through and »around« the broadcasting of such films (or in this case, the publication of a novel by a well-known TV actress, comedian and screenwriter), seems justified. Regarding the transnational communicative figuration which has formed around the theme of reproductive tourism, split parenthood and commercial surrogacy in India, I found two aspects in the newspaper articles about the novel quite telling. First, that some authors expected the novel to be adapted for a feature film very soon and also mentioned the fact that Syal already had an eye on the film rights when her book was published.[35] Second, Syal also mentioned in one interview that it was in fact a BBC documentary which inspired her to write the book[36]; after watching this documentary, she says that she knew immediately what her third novel would be about, and there can be hardly any doubt that Syal was referring to the documentary »House of Surrogates« (2013) made by direc-

---

35   Susan Elkin (2015). »The House of Hidden Mothers, by Meera Syal - Book Review: An Anglo-Indian Fiction With Hard Truths Lurking Beneath, Screaming Out to be Made into a Film«, *The Independent*. June 20, 2015.

36   See for instance the BBC TV interview »Meera Syal on India's Surrogacy Industry«, published online on June 02, 2015.

tor Matt Rudge. Rudge's film »House of Surrogates« features fertility specialist Dr. Nayana Patel from Gujarat very prominently. Patel is surrounded in the picture below by »her surrogates«, as she likes to call them in interviews. She became instantly famous all over the world after the screening of Lisa Ling's report about her clinic on the Oprah Winfrey Show in 2007 and was subsequently treated like a spokesperson for the Indian surrogacy industry by international media. It is not difficult at all to imagine who the model for the renowned fertility specialist in Meera Syal's novel must have been:

> Then there's Dr Passi, the internationally respected doctor who convinces herself, and half convinces the reader, that she is providing a service which overseas couples want while giving Indian women the chance to improve their lot and educate their children - as she funds her own Western lifestyle and puts her own three children through medical school. Is it advantageous for all concerned or is she simply an unscrupulous exploiter? (Susan Elkin, »The House of Hidden Mothers«, by Meera

Syal - Book Review: An Anglo-Indian Fiction With Hard Truths Lurking Beneath«, *Independent online.* June 20, 2015).

Image 2: Still from the BBC documentary »House of Surrogates« (Source of image: http://www.bbc.co.uk/programmes/b03c591s - last accessed Sep 06, 2019).

In an article published in August 2017 in the *The Guardian,* the author Ellen E. Jones ponders about the question why infertility, parenthood and surrogacy have become such prominent features in a number of highly successful TV productions recently, most notably Jane Campion's »Top of the Lake: The China Girl« and a series based on Margaret Atwood's novel »The Handmaid's Tale« (1985) which was adapted for television under the same title in 2017[37]. In spite of the fact that the article explores television's most recent »obsession with surrogate mothers«, a longer section of it is actually about the reception and long-lasting impact of the before mentioned BBC documentary from 2013.

Director Matt Rudge says in the same article that when he first visited Dr. Patel's fertility clinic in Anand he thought that viewers would have impulsive reactions and Jones agrees that »House of Surrogates« depiction of a vast global wealth gap, as well as the careless way the bonds of baby and birth mother were severed, remained upsetting. In the years following the screening of Rudge's influential documentary, Nayana Patel's Akanksha infertility clinic has become the central visual symbol of a permanent surveillance of surrogate mothers in the so-called surrogacy hostels in Anand where they have to spend a large part of their pregnancy. The »visual overrepresentation« of Dr. Nayana Patel and her Akanksha fertility clinic in Anand is the most obvious evidence for the borrowings and intertextual references between different films and media formats which add to the establishment and reiteration of more or less »standardized« stories and framings.

III. Living and Laboring Under a Panoptic Gaze

Although this does not apply to all the contexts and cities in India where surrogate mothers sometimes stay at home during their pregnancy, the first association and indeed a standard visual representation of surrogate mothers in documentaries - as well as in feature films - is the dormitory of the surrogacy hostels.[38] The constant surveillance and immobilization of surrogate mothers who are separated from their own families and children for a long time has been the focus of much critique in the academic discussion as well as in public debates.[39] However, this narrative is also sometimes compli-

---

37   Ellen E. Jones (2017). »Empty Nests: Why Has TV Become Obsessed With Surrogate Mothers?« *The Guardian*. August 14, 2017.

38   Ishani K. Dutta's 2011 documentary film »Womb on Rent«, is one of the few films in which the surrogate completes a large part of the gestational period at home in Delhi with her family.

39   Anindita Majumdar also describes the differences between housing practices in Anand, Mumbai and Delhi: »[T]he lack of enthusiasm amongst agents and doctors to house the surrogate with her own family during the period of gestation is based on ideas of hygiene, home atmosphere and proper diet. In Anand, Gujarat

cated by surrogates themselves who talk about the strong bonds of friendship and solidarity between women who share a lot of similar experiences,

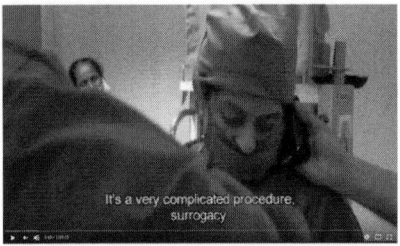 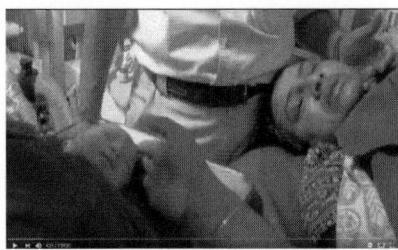

Images 3 and 4: Two stills from »Google Baby«. The left image shows Dr. Patel responding to a potential client on the phone while finishing a cesarean section on a surrogate in her clinic. The image on the right shows the surrogate mother briefly touching the newborn child while Dr. Patel tells the nurse to take »the baby out to the mother« (»Google Baby«, 3:40 min and 4:21 min).

or about the little subversive acts they perform together to undermine the medical control over their bodies (Pande 2010). »Ma Na Sapna - A Mother's Dream« (2013) by Austrian director Valerie Gudenus has several interesting scenes in this regard in which we see and hear, on the one hand, how inter-personal conflicts between surrogates may erupt in the claustrophobic and barrack-like atmosphere of the surrogacy hostel. On the other hand, we listen to personal stories such as Champa's (33:18min) who, four days after the embryo transfer into her womb, tells the director's team and interpreter Reshma Jain how much she hopes that the results will be positive (i.e. that she will be pregnant), not least because she is visibly enjoying the company of her two roommates whom she likes a lot. Also, by hearing Champa comment on how much cooler the house (hostel) is during the hot season, we may be inclined to believe that, despite the constant surveillance, (self-)disciplining and immobilization, at least for some surrogates, this could indeed be a welcome break from their strenuous and demanding everyday lives. Interestingly but perhaps not surprisingly, this ambivalent trope of a »welcome holiday« for the surrogates whose lives outside the hostel might be so much tougher than inside the clinic, is also taken up in fictional formats (see Chap. 3 in this volume).

---

and Mumbai where the practice of surrogate hostels is actively endorsed and followed - surrogates' families are constructed as 'dysfunctional spaces' with non-cooperative husbands and inlaws. But in Delhi most of the surrogate mothers lived in their own homes with their families during the pregnancy«. (Majumdar, 2014b: 208).

A very problematic aspect is the camera's gaze onto the laboring bodies of surrogate mothers during childbirth, an ethically questionable visualization of surrogacy which has nevertheless rarely been discussed nor problematized. Their faces covered with sweat and sometimes tears, the surrogates usually do not speak. It is once again the doctor in charge or other 'observing medical experts' who speaks for her, interprets and comments on the situation. It is of course a golden opportunity for the filmmaker: an extremely versatile doctor performing a routine c-section while responding to a phone call and saying a few friendly words towards the surrogate mother as well as the camera. Then, very matter-of-factly, Dr. Patel announces »Now we send the baby out to the mother« (»Google Baby«, 4:35 min). What better opportunity could there be for a filmmaker than this moment of twofold delivery in order to convey the complexities of split motherhood and the commodification of bodies and babies?

IV. Framing Surrogacy as Labor vs. a Prevalent Rhetoric of »Rented Wombs«

One standardized narrative which was first introduced to a global audience by the Oprah Winfrey Show in 2007 and has been reiterated since then in many documentary films and countless other media, is the metaphor of the »womb for rent« or »rented womb« of the surrogate mother. Specifically with regard to the coverage in Indian news media, Anindita Majumdar notes an important shift taking place between 2007 and 2014 in the way surrogacy was perceived vis-à-vis the infertile couple and their individual »drama of childlessness«, which ultimately led to an almost complete erasure of the surrogate mother from the picture (Majumdar 2014a). She argues that the exploitative business of surrogacy, the missing legal regulation and the many risks involved for surrogate mothers were now increasingly couched in a language of altruism and philanthropy and framed as a »win-win-situation« or an act of solidarity between two women - one woman whose longing for a genetic child would be fulfilled and the other woman whose hopes for a better future for her children would finally become real. However, this »rhetoric of the womb« is by no means limited to the framing and coverage in Indian news media, but can equally be regarded as a key metaphor which is used transnationally in the context of almost every media-related discussion of commercial surrogacy in India and other countries in the so-called global South. In view of this erasure of the surrogate mother from the media coverage, the increasing use of a rhetoric of the womb as well as a general shift of attention to the plight of the childless couple, it is particularly relevant to find out in how far documentary filmmakers are motivated and able to »step in« and help enhance the visibility or give voice to the surrogate workers through their films. In many documentaries, the surrogates can only be interviewed inside the fertility clinic or inside the hostels and it is hence no surprise that they often display a deep gratitude towards the clinic and especially towards the doctor in charge. They also tend to reproduce the same rhetoric of altruism and of surrogacy being a »life changing opportunity« for them which, as the audience is often made to believe, will allow them to buy a house or invest the money they earn for a better education of their children. However, it is interesting how a film like *Ma Na Sapna* brings this into question, rather subtly. On the one hand, there can be no doubt that in many scenes in this film, Nayana Patel once again knows how to make use of a documentary film for her tried and tested mode of self-representation. But *Ma Na Sapna* also manages to qualify some of the statements which had been made in previous documentaries on the Akanksha fertility clinic and commercial surrogacy in India in general, such as the assertion that surrogate mothers will be able to buy a house for their family from the money they earn for their physical and emotional labor. Some dialogues in Valerie Gudenus' film make it very clear that the prices for houses have gone up very quickly in all the surrounding localities, while the wage Dr. Patel's clinic is willing to pay to the surrogate mothers has not been increased correspondingly during the last couple of years.

Despite the fact that visualizations of the dormitories have become a standardized form of representation of commercial surrogacy in India, it can be argued, that precisely this kind of visualization enables us, the viewers, to see and immediately understand why the rhetoric of rented wombs is so deeply problematic. Not only because it serves to further erase the surrogate from the picture, but also because it suggests that no active labor is involved in the whole process, as the surrogate seemingly only »rents out« a body part, her uterus, and is hence not seen as a worker who is, accordingly, also entitled to labor rights and social security. Indeed, many of the documentaries on reproductive tourism and commercial surrogacy in India help us understand that surrogate workers engage in both, emotional as well as intimate labor. They are thus also refuting the notion brought forward by Eileen Boris and Rhacel Salazar Parreñas that »surrogate mothers do not engage in emotional labor, though their jobs may involve emotional labor that would occur in private and not public spaces«:

> However, emotional labor is not a prerequisite or requirement in intimate labor. In many cases, intimate laborers need not regulate their emotions. Sperm donors, (...)

and surrogate mothers do not engage in emotional labor (Boris and Salazar Parreñas, 2010: 7).

It is questionable whether the public-private binary can be applied either to
the peculiar space of the surrogacy hostel or to the mediated communicative
space in which face-to-face labor is indeed involved and surrogate workers
have to display certain emotions to induce a particular feeling in the client
or customer, in this case, the commissioning parents. This is, for instance,
aptly illustrated in the opening scene from Surabhi Sharma's 2013 documentary »Can We See the Baby Bump Please?« We get introduced to the
mediated kinning practices of a commissioning couple from the US who
through their routine Skype calls try hard to »connect« with the unborn child
and also to engage in some small talk with the surrogate mother Haseena.
She does not speak or understand English, hence the help of an ever-smiling
interpreter is required not only to translate words but also to provide a connection between the two distant lifeworlds. Nevertheless, it is Haseena who
is expected to »perform« a happy and healthy pregnancy in front of the
computer screen, to show her growing belly and also, to display an interest
in the commissioning parents' favourite music that they would like her - or
rather, the baby inside her belly - to listen to. In short, Haseena's labor goes
far beyond providing a body part and caring for herself as well as for the
unborn baby in her womb.

Outlook

Journalistic and academic articles have so far mostly addressed documentary films on transnational reproduction and commercial surrogacy in India
as individual texts, generally focusing more on the content than on the form
of the films and hence, often also neglecting the origin(s) and itineraries of
certain images, tropes or recurring visual representations. This chapter was
based on the assumption that it is not only interesting but also academically
relevant to trace some of these image itineraries to understand how they
might contribute to emerging global imaginaries (Brosius and Wenzelhue-
mer 2011) as well as to a translocal communicative figuration around the
topic of transnational reproduction and commercial surrogacy in India.
Looking at a number of very successful documentaries that were made primarily for transnational audiences between 2009-2013 and by filmmakers
who are mostly located outside India, it sought to shed light specifically on
three images and tropes that it considers central for this communicative figuration: 1) the medical authority-cum-media actor (i.e. internationally well-

known fertility expert and doctor in charge, Dr. Nayana Patel), 2) the image of the surrogacy hostels and dormitories in Anand, Gujarat (i.e. the deeply ambivalent trope of a »welcome holiday« for the surrogates vs. »panoptic surveillance and control« of their bodies, actions and thoughts) and 3) the contested notion of »rented wombs« (i.e. the passive provision of a body part) vs. surrogacy as labor (including very demanding and complex intimate as well as emotional labor). The chapter showed that the flows of these images and tropes are by no means restricted to intertextual references between the documentaries in focus here, but that they travel across a wide variety of different media, contexts and formats, including for instance, television dramas, talk shows, newspaper interviews, documentary theatre, journalistic travel photography and novels. It can thus be argued that conceptualizations of individual media as decisive »channels« of a successful mediation and subsequent societal debate about technological innovations and related changes of practices of social reproduction and »doing family«, need to be complemented by approaches which focus more on the »patterns of processes of communicative interweaving that exist across various media and have a thematic framing that orients communicative action« (Hasebrink and Hepp, 2013: 10, as cited in: Radde-Antweiler, 2018: 210f.).

In addition to focusing on the emergence of transmedial communicative figurations and thematic framings that actually define »the topic«, however, it is also important to identify and illuminate the critical absences within these communicative spaces. One such critical aspect is the underrepresentation of Indian intending parents in documentary films on surrogacy which adds to the notion that most commissioning parents are from the global North or Western countries. This is - or at least before the ban on surrogacy in India - was not the case, as Sarojini Nadimpally and Deepa Venkatachalam from the SAMA resource group for women and health in Delhi point out. According to their research, there is an »equally large number of Indians who are 'consumers' of ARTs and surrogacy« (Nadimpally and Venkatachalam, 2016: 91). But while foreign clients usually access clinics in the metropolitan and bigger cities in India, clinics in small towns and cities are primarily frequented by so-called local consumers. Documentaries (both international as well as by Indian filmmakers) which do not focus on Anand are mostly shot in Mumbai or Delhi, however, so that the dominance of urban-centered representations may have added to the wrong perception that commercial surrogacy and split parenthood is largely an urban or metropolitan phenomenon in India. As documentaries are an important reference for academic articles and sometimes also an inspiration for future research projects, this also means that in addition to an already rich theoretical discussion about North-South inequalities and India as an exemplary »labor market primarily for the reproduction of the biological and affective life of *other places*« (Vora 2015: 7; emphasis my own), a theoretical inquiry into the socio-spatial dynamics within the »same places« is required.

References

BBC TV (2015). »Meera Syal on India's Surrogacy Industry«, published online on June 02, 2015. Online available at: http/::www.bbc.com/news/av/entertainments-arts-32974891/meera-syal-on-india-s-surrogacy-industry (last accessed Aug 14, 2019).

Bennett, James and Strange, Nikki (Eds.)(2011). *Television as Digital Media*. Durham, NC: Duke University Press.

Bernard, Andreas (2014). Kinder machen. Neue Reproduktionstechnologien und die Ordnung der Familie. Samenspende, Leihmütter, Künstliche Befruchtung. Frankfurt am Main: Fischer.

Bharadwaj, Aditya (2012). »The Other Mother: Supplementary Wombs and the Surrogate State in India«. In: Knecht, Michi; Klotz, Maren and Beck, Stefan (Eds.). *Reproductive Technologies as a Global Form. Ethnographies of Knowledge, Practices and Transnational Encounters*. Frankfurt am Main/New York: Campus. 139-160.

Boris, Eileen and Parreñas, Rhacel Salazar (2010)(Eds.). *Intimate Labors: Cultures, Technologies, and the Politics of Care*. Stanford, CA: Stanford University Press.

Brosius, Christiane and Wenzlhuemer, Roland (2011). *Transcultural Turbulences. Towards a Multi-Sited Reading of Image Flows*. Berlin: Springer. 3-24.

Cooper, M. (2008). *Life as Surplus*. Seattle: University of Washington Press.

Elkin, Susan (2015). »The House of Hidden Mothers, by Meera Syal – Book Review: An Anglo-Indian Fiction with Hard Truths Lurking Beneath, Screaming Out to be Made Into a Film«, *The Independent*. June 20, 2015. Online available at: https://www.independent.co.uk/arts-entertainment/books/reviews/the-house-of-hidden-mothers-by-meera-syal-book-review-an-anglo-indian-fiction-with-hard-truths-10300266.html (last acceseed Aug 14, 2019).

Green, Alon-Lee (2015). »Where Is the Concern for the Surrogate Mothers in Nepal? « *Haaretz*. April 27, 2015. Online available at: https://www.haaretz.com/opinion/.premium-what-about-the-surrogates-in-nepal-1.5355284 (last accessed Aug 14, 2019).

Gross, Aeyal (2015). »It Takes an Earthquake in Nepal to Talk About Surrogacy in Israel«. *Haaretz*. April 30, 2015. Online available at: https://www.haaretz.com/.premium-shaking-up-surrogacy-in-israel-1.5356019 (last accessed Aug 14, 2019).

Hepp, Andreas (2013). »The Communicative Figurations of Mediatized Worlds: Mediatization Research in Times of the 'Mediation of Everything«. Published online at: https://www.kommunikative-figurationen.de/fileadmin/user_upload/Arbeitspapiere/CoFi_EWP_No-1_Hepp.pdf (last accessed August 14, 2019).

Hvidtfeldt Madsen, Karen (2015). »Documentaries on Transnational Surrogacy in India:

Questions of Privilege, Respectability and Kinship«. In: In Kr's, Charlotte and Myong, Lene et al. (Eds.) *Critical Kinship Studies*. Rowman & Littlefield International. 117-132.

Jones, Ellen E. (2017). »Empty Nests: Why Has TV Become Obsessed With Surrogate Mothers?« *The Guardian.* August 14, 2017. Online available at: https://www.theguardian.com/tv-and-radio/2017/aug/14/top-of-the-lake-handmaids-tale-tv-obsessed-surrogate-mothers-infertility-parenting (last accessed Aug 14, 2019).

Klein Leichman, Abigail (2011). »The Israeli Mom Behind Google Baby«. *Israel21.* Oct 27, 2011. Online available at: https://www.israel21c.org/the-israeli-mom-behind-google-baby/ (last accessed Aug 14, 2019).

Majumdar, Anindita (2014a). »The Rhetoric of the Womb: The Representation of Surrogacy in India's Popular Mass Media«. In: DasGupta, Sayantani and Das Dasgupta, Shamita (eds.). *Globalization and Transnational Surrogacy in India: Outsourcing Life*. Lanham, Boulder a.o.: Lexington Books. 107-124.

---. (2014b). »Nurturing an Alien Pregnancy: Surrogate Mothers, Intended Parents and Disembodied Relationships«. *Indian Journal of Gender Studies* 21(2): 199-224.

Mitra, Sayani and Hansen, Solveig (2015). »Auf der anderen Seite der Kamera. Leihmutterschaft in Indien und das moralische Anliegen der Dokumentarfilmerin Surabhi Sharma«. *Ethik in der Medizin* 27(1): 69-80.

Nadimpally, Sarojini and Venkatachalam, Deepa (2016). Marketing Reproduction: Assisted Reproductive Technologies and Commercial Surrogacy in India. *Indian Journal of Gender Studies* 23(1): 87-104.

Pande, Amrita (2014). *Wombs in Labor. Transnational Commercial Surrogacy in India.* New York: Columbia University Press.

---. (2010). »Commercial Surrogacy in India: Manufacturing a Perfect Mother-Worker«. *Signs* 35(4): 969-992.

Radde-Antweiler, Kerstin (2018). »How to Study Religion and Video Gaming: A Critical Discussion«. In: Šisler, Vít; Radde-Antweiler, Kerstin and Zeiler, Xenia (Eds.). *Methods for Studying Video Games and Religion*. London/New York: Routledge. 210-214.

Rajan, K. S. (2006). *Biocapital*. Durham: Duke Univesity Press.

Rose, N. (2001). »The Politics of Life Itself«. *Theory, Culture and Society* 18(6): 1-30.

Rudrappa, Sharmla (2017). »In India, Commercial Surrogacy Continues Despite Ban. Instead of Banning Commercial Surrogacy, Countries Should Regulate the Practice to Better Protect the Birth Mother from Exploitation«. *U.S. News*, Oct 26, 2017. Online available at: https://www.us-news.com/news/best-countries/articles/2017-10-26/in-india-clinics-find-loopholes-to-banned-commercial-surrogacy (last accessed Sep 06, 2018, the source is no longer available).

Schneider, Nadja-Christina (2018). »Crossmedia Flows of Documentary Images and the Transnational Communicative Figuration Surrounding Gestational Surrogacy in India«. *BioScope: South Asian Screen Studies* 9(2): 1-24.

Sessions, Samel Yancey (2012). »Made in India. A Film About Surrogacy«. *Journal of the American Medical Association* 308(8): 818-819.

Sorensen, Inge (2013). *Documentary in a Multiplatform Context*. Online available at: https://www.researchgate.net/publication/281015085_Documentary_in_a_ Multiplatform_Context (last accessed Aug 14, 2019).

Strathern, Marilyn (2002). »Still Giving Nature a Helping Hand? Surrogacy: A Debate About Technology and Society«. *Journal of Molecular Biology* 319(4): 985-993.

Unkown author (2013). »Surrogacy Was Our Last Resort«. *India Today*, July 22, 2013. Online available at: https://www.indiatoday.in/magazine/special-re port/story/20130722-aamir-khan-azad-kiran-rao-surrogacy-764710-1999-11-30 (last accessed Aug 14, 2019).

Unknown author (2016). »Supermom of State, Sushma Swaraj, Gifts India a Sanskari Surrogacy Bill. Only Married Indian Citizen Couples Can Opt for 'Altruistic Surro-gacy', But Not Our Singles, LGBTQ of Those in Live-in Relationships«. *DailyO*, Aug, 24 2016. Online available at: https://www.dailyo.in/politics/surrogacy-bill-sushma-swaraj-reproductive-rights-womens-rights-commercial-surrogacy-celebri-ties-lgbtq-single-parent/story/1/12559.html (last accessed Aug 14, 2019).

Vora, Kalindi (2015). *Life Support. Biocapital And The New History of Outsourced La-bor*. Minneapolis, MN: University of Minnesota Press.

Vora, Priyanka (2017). »Surrogacy in India: Parliamantary Committee Reopens the Sur-rogacy Debate, Says Commercial Surrogacy Should be Allowed«. *Scroll.in*. August 17, 2017. Online available at: https://scroll.in/pulse/847458/parliamentary-commit-tee-reopens-the-surrogacy-debate-says-commercial-surrogacy-debate-should-be-allowed (last accessed Aug 14, 2019).

Waldby, C. (2002). *The Visible Human Project*. London: Routledge.

Films

Can We See the Baby Bump Please? (2013, 49min). Directed by Surabhi Sharma. Pro-duced by Sama - Resource Group for Women and Health. DVD: Magic Lantern Mov-ies.

Google Baby (2009, 76min). Directed by Zippi Brand Frank. Online available at: https://www.youtube.com/watch?v=pQGlAM0iWFM (last accessed Aug 14, 2019).

House of Surrogates (2013, 90min). Directed by Matt Rudge for the BBC.

Made in India (2010, 95min). Directed by Rebecca Haimowitz and Vaishali Sinha. DVD.

Ma Na Sapna - A Mother's Dream (2013, 86min). Directed by Valerie Gudenus. DVD: Journeyman Pictures.

Mother Anonymous (2011, 10min). Directed by Rahul Ranadive. Unpublished DVD.

Womb on Rent (2013, 49min). Directed by Ishani K. Dutta. Online available at: https://www.youtube.com/watch?v=Hf_hA_mY6X8 (last accessed Sep 06, 2018).

Wombs for Rent in India (2015, 26min). Directed by and produced for Russia Today.

Online available at: https://www.youtube.com/watch?v=PSXZSdMmRdg (last accessed Aug 14, 2019).

Chapter 3: Repro-Dramas on Screen: Mediating Surrogacy, Split Motherhood and Reproductive Tourism to German Television Audiences

Nadja-Christina Schneider

Introduction

Image 1: Screenschot from the film *River of Life - Born on the Banks of Ganges*

I can see your skepticism quite clearly, Mr. Hansen. But, unfortunately, your Western standards do not apply here. All of our surrogate mothers grant infertile women the world over the joys of motherhood. And they are paid well for it. Enough to facilitate a new life. They really do make good money. And apart from that, we help them set up their own livelihoods. It is a win-win situation and - contrary to your own country's legislation - perfectly legal in India.

With this monologue, the director of a fertility clinic in Varanasi and doctor in charge, Dr. Rohini,[40] opens the conversation with her visitor from Germany, Robert Hansen, in the TV drama *River of Life - Born on the Banks of*

---

40   Bengali actress Swarupa Ghosh is known to Indian audiences as Peeshi Ma in the film *Vicky Donor* (2012), a surprise hit dealing with anonymous sperm donation, and to German audiences in her role as doctor in charge of a fertility clinic in Kolkata in the television production *Monsoon Baby* (2014).

Ganges (2017). Robert does not approach Dr. Rohini as a potential intended father - he is looking for a child whom his late sister had commissioned by an Indian surrogate two years prior. Assuming his sister's genetic child (her ovum and the sperm of a donor from Germany) was inevitably a member of his family, he now, together with his mother, wants to take the girl »home«. By the end of this just under 90 minutes long *river movie*, however, will have reconsidered his claim on the child as well as his early thoughts and feelings on family and kinship at the beginning of his stay in India.

At the end of February 2016, as the month-long film shooting in Varanasi began, the Indian government had already outlawed any form of commercial surrogacy in India for four months and had concurrently announced a draft bill which was to facilitate, so-called, altruistic surrogacy exclusively for childless heterosexual couples with Indian citizenship who had been married for a minimum of five years.[41] Whilst the German television crew was struggling with their set-up in Varanasi - most of the crew had never been to India before - and was trying to finish the shoot to the best of their ability, the ban on commercial surrogacy and its impact on ongoing transnational 'commissions', the surrogates themselves, and also on Indian society in general was discussed as intensely and controversially as seldom before in the Indian public (see Schneider 2018).

How much of these current debates and recent legal developments on the ground can, and should, a film about surrogacy in India, which was filmed locally and quite laboriously for the German public service broadcasting authorities, convey to its target audiences? Was the film crew able, or even interested, to take notice in order to inform audiences during the inevitable press junkets, at least superficially, on the present situation in India?

These questions might come as a surprise, after all, this movie is not a documentary or reportage but a feature film in a series titled 'Cinema of Hearts' which was broadcast on a Sunday night in February 2017 as a competitor on ZDF[42] - the very same time slot during which the largest market

---

41 The draft bill came as a surprise, as many women's rights organisations had long waited and advocated for a stricter legal regulation of what has hitherto been a largely unregulated reproductive market, but not for a complete ban of commercial surrogacy in India (see Chap. 3 in this volume). The Surrogacy (Regulation) Bill was passed in August 2019.

42 In terms of total viewing market share, the two biggest public service broadcasting channels ZDF and ARD (now also called »Das Erste«) continue to hold their dominant position, closely followed by the two commercial channels RTL and SAT 1.

share is week by week ensnared by the popular detective series *Tatort* on ARD. In fact, the film reached 4.4 million viewers during its television premiere on February 5th, 2017, which corresponds to a market share of 11.9% for this evening, quite an achievement for a Sunday night.[43] Advertising and PR strategies were devised around the public image of the Iranian-born German leading actor Pegah Ferydoni. Correspondingly, the actor gave a series of extensive interviews and was invited to talk shows in order to report on India, surrogacy, her own motherhood and her experiences during the filming on location. In view of the competitive and profoundly changing nature of national and transnational television production, it is becoming crucial to raise interest in essential issues through credible testimonials, 'authentic' actors or other 'experts' and to communicate stories which inform and engage audiences in an equally entertaining and instructive manner. Against this background, the question of the role of the production and knowledge transfer through - and perhaps around the broadcasting of such films - seems justified. Although converging media technologies have generated new media forms which greatly changed the viewing patterns and practices of audiences, television in its (roughly) usual mode does persist alongside these developments and still reaches a large percentage of the population in countries such as Germany. Media routines generally exhibit hard-wearing perseverance as the phenomenon of the firmly established Sunday night detective drama on German public service broadcasting showcases. Meanwhile, most of these routines are nevertheless embedded within profoundly transformed media environments and actions, which would render the conventional single media approach of past decades problematic at best.

Communicating Split Motherhood and Surrogacy in India AcrossDifferent 'Domains of Knowledge'

In the past years, groundbreaking ethnographic research on surrogacy in India, and partially also related interventions in public debates, were conducted, amongst others, by Amrita Pande (2014), Anandita Majumdar (2013) and Daisy Deomampo (2016). Beyond commercial surrogacy in India, the theoretical exploration of this complex and widely ramified research field has also significantly been shaped by key publications by Marcia Inhorn (2015), Michi Knecht et al. (2012), Jyotsna Agnihotri Gupta (2012),

---

43   The film was available on demand via the broadcaster's streaming services until May 2017 and now occasionally pops up on YouTube.

Arlie Hochschild (2012) and Kalindi Vora (2009) - to name just a few important scholars in this growing transdisicplinary research field. In addition to that, several documentary films have been produced on the topic, which are received in most diverse contexts and therefore substantially contribute to the knowledge transfer and discussion of the societal implications of split mother- and parenthood, as well as on questions concerning transnational reproductive markets across very different 'domains of knowledge' (Strathern 2002). Generally overlooked in academic publications, however, are as of yet fictional formats (specifically short films or feature films) and, most of all, the knowledge surrounding them in a communicative figuration (Hepp 2013: 10) which is marked by the thematic frame of split motherhood and reproductive tourism in India. To explore the question of how this communicative figuration, formed by announced or already televised films, took shape transmedially, is what motivates this article. Arguably, the reproduction of stereotypical images of India which are firmly established in German visual traditions of depiction, leads in conjunction with the subjects of pregnancy, motherhood, birth as well as pre- and neonatal medical care to a virtually new Eurocentric imagery of fear, which especially *Monsoon Baby* (2014), the second film discussed below, devises to great dramatic effect. Moreover, the powerful transnational effect of the critical media event *Nirbhaya* or *Delhi Gang Rape Case* (see Schneider and Titzmann 2014) is strongly evident in the depictions of physical and verbal violence against women in the two television dramas, especially by husbands, and this adds seamlessly to German media coverages and general perceptions of India since 2012/13 which are dominated by the topoi of violence against, and disregard of, women and girls in India.[44] I am certainly not attempting to relativize the problem of gender inequality and gender based violence in India, but rather want to point to the problematic nature of these renewed central topoi and essentialising tele-visualisations of India in the past years. In this context, it is also important to reflect on the visual consumption of violence and of tales of violence from other*ed* cultures.

In spite of this critique, it can be argued that both films *River of Life - Born on the Banks of Ganges* (2017) as well as *Monsoon Baby* (2014), and the cross-media communications around them centralise the question of the

---

44   For an analysis and nuanced discussion of the asymmetry of knowledge and 'potent convergence of »ignorance« and »instant access« that new technologies have made possible', see Maitrayee Chaudhuri's excellent article 'National and Global Media Discourse after the savage death of »Nirbhaya«: Instant Access and Unequal Knowledge' (Chaudhuri 2015: 19-44).

renegotiation of family, motherhood and kinship, specifically in view of already prevalent societal transformations due to technological innovations. The scale of these transformative processes is, thus, made visible and comprehensible for a larger audience, which, following Strathern, might indeed contribute to societal self-reflection.

Visualizing Split Parenthood - Negotiating Normative Motherhood and Kinship

Images 2 & 3 Screenshots from the film *River of Live - Born on the Banks of Ganges*

The very first scene of the television film *River of Life - Born on the Banks of Ganges* shows a young woman, Parvati, walking quickly along the ghats of Varanasi. At her side is a little blonde, light-skinned girl whom she calls Suri. The girl attracts a lot of attention due to her striking appearance, much to Paravati's displeasure. The young woman, however, is treated like an outcast, she lives separated from her husband and relatives in an informal settlement along the river banks close to a busy rail- and motorway bridge (Rajghat, Varanasi). Parvati tries to support herself and Suri as best as she can and treats the child very lovingly and sensitively. Yet shortly thereafter, her evidently violent (ex-)husband, Ganesh, will kidnap Suri from out of their tent and take the child away across the Ganges in a small boat. In the moment of departure, he yells at his (ex-)wife that she, »the whore with the bastard child«, should be glad to start a new life without Suri somewhere, far away, where nobody knew of her shame.

Even though from a critical feminist standpoint both phenomena can be and - taking necessary worker's rights and social recognition under consideration - probably should be regarded as physical and emotional labour, the close association of prostitution and surrogacy is highly problematic in this

specific context.[45] Ganesh insulting his (ex-)wife Parvati by calling her a
»whore« and Suri a »bastard child« conveys to television audiences in Germany that he, as a poor and little educated man, has no knowledge whatsoever of assisted reproductive medicine. He seems neither aware that sexual
contact has seized to be requisite for procreation for quite some time now,
nor that the globally predominant form of commercial surrogacy of two
decades does not intend any kind of genetic relations between the surrogate
and the planned child. He appears ignorant of the fact that the fertilised egg,
which was implanted in her womb is, hence, either a donor's or the commissioning mother's own.

How Parvati, on the other hand, gained these insights and the necessary
offer to work as a surrogate remains unanswered in the film. She also does
not state the frequently cited hopes of affording a better education for her
own children, or an apartment for her family, as motivational. Rather, she
claims that she had done it for her own good - in the hopes of funding a
decent education, of acquiring ICT skills and finding a good job. But then,
the German commissioning mother never came to 'collect' Suri and she
found herself in the unforeseen role of a single parent in most adverse conditions. Yet, this role comes easy to Parvati, whose name was surely not
picked coincidentally by the screenwriters, even though Suri is not her own
'genetic' child. Later in the film, she will say that Suri is her daughter, that
she had given birth to her, and that the girl belonged with her. »Suri is a
child of the Ganges«, she says (44:35).

Dressed in a shirt and tie and carrying a briefcase, Robert Hansen appears
to be on his daily commute to work and not a tourist in the middle of Varanasi. His attire, strained expression and poise instantly illustrate his discomfort outside of his accustomed cultural context and beg the question if, under
less pressing circumstances, he had ever been inclined to visit a country as

---

45   Unbeknownst of the abilities of reproductive technologies to split mother- and
parenthood, as of the dispensability of sexual contact, the stigma of 'prostitution'
- that they had 'sold' their bodies - still weighs heavily on many surrogates in
India. The topos of surrogacy as a form of prostitution is also reminiscent of
films such as *Chori Chori, Chupke Chupke* (2001), in which Preity Zinta plays
a prostitute who offers her services as a surrogate to a couple pressured to procreate. The child whom she gives up is genetically her own and was conceived
'naturally'. Preity's character, Madhu, unfortunately also fell in love with the intended father, Raj (played by Salman Khan). At the end she rejects payment for
the surrogacy and leaves with her head held high. Recalling this particular film,
which - in the context of already establishing translocal reproductive markets at
that time appeared more than anachronistic - in the light of the current debate in
India and the new legal restrictions on 'altruistic' surrogacy (solely for married,
heterosexual Indian citizens), however, is not devoid of a certain irony.

unfamiliar to him as India. But then again, there is this serious matter which has prompted him and his mother to their journey: Only two years after her death it came to light, rather coincidentally, that his late sister had, as a single woman with the help of an anonymous sperm donation in Germany, commissioned a surrogate mother in Varanasi. Due to the commissioning mother's sudden death, however, the girl, Suri, could not be picked up from Dr. Rohini's clinic after birth and therefore remained with the surrogate mother, Parvati.

Images 4 and 5: Screenshots from the film *River of Life - Born on the Banks of Ganges.*

Now, who is to lay claim on Suri - the genetically related 'uncle' Robert and 'grandma' from Germany, or rather the not genetically related surrogate, Parvati, who had carried Suri to term for the deceased commissioning mother, raised her, and consequently considers herself the child's mother? In how far does the, in the German context readily quoted, well-being of the child factor into these negotiations between the parties involved? To Robert and his mother the case is quite clear, at least initially: the child 'belongs' to them and, had they only known of her existence earlier, two years would not have passed for them to take Suri to Germany. Now that they consider themselves on the brink of taking 'their' grandchild and niece 'home' - indeed, they do not know the girl and have never seen her before, yet - one thing Robert knows for sure: »we will change that name again« (14:54 min). Before today's possibility of a so-called half-open or open adoption, when the incognito-adoption was still the norm in the Federal Republic of Germany - that is, adopting parents and adopted children could only obtain information on, let alone contact, the biological mother and family with great difficulty - it was common and even officially recommended that no affiliation should, or rather had, to be maintained with this former history and identity.[46] The symbolic and performative expression of this desired attempt at forgetting or erasing the pre-adoptive history of the children was an official name change. The child was expected to henceforth identify with and grow into this new given name. Thus, many adopted adults in Germany, who were given to families by incognito adoption and were either only able to obtain fragmented or, in the frequent case of document destruction by the German authorities, no information at all on their birth mothers and extended families, are unaware that they used to be called by a completely different name - whether by their biological mothers or the children's home staff. This practice of rarely questioned name change is echoed clearly in Robert's statement through which he expresses his claim to the child and simultaneously his latent anxiety about the child's possible 'character' before being absorbed into his family. Consequently, he considers Parvati's 'task' as accomplished and assures her that he and his mother, »will cover her expenses and pay her for all her troubles« (25:20 min). Their attitude, however, will shift fundamentally in the course of the film as Robert joins Paravati in the search for Suri, possibly falls in love with her, and, at least partially, agrees to engage with the country and contexts unfamiliar to him. Suri, nevertheless, is given another name (Amy), if only temporarily, as Ganesh sells the kidnapped girl to a US American couple in search of an adoptive child. The couple is apparently unaware, or probably unwilling to question, what sorts of criminal machinations have granted their wish - they are far too pleased to have finally realised their vision of family by the way of a longed-for child. But their joy and self-deception is short-lived, as Robert 'rescues' Suri on leaving the country, Ganesh is overpowered, and Parvati simply picks up 'her' child in the midst of the confusion and runs off with the girl. Yet again Robert goes off in search, only to finally realise that Suri belongs with 'her' mother and should grow up in India. Framed by an

---

46   The Ministry of Family Affairs, Senior Citizen, Women and Youth states on its website: « In principle, the law provides for the form of the incognito option. In the incognito adoption, the parents do not know the adopters and there is no contact. Through incognito, the founding of the new family is to be protected from the influence of biological parents and relatives and the child from a feeling of being torn between the biological and accepting parents. However, the biological parents always have the possibility to deposit letters, pictures or similar for the child. These documents are then kept in the adoption mediation files. With the consent of all parties involved and in the case of advocacy and support by the mediation office, the incognito can be lifted at any time, so that there is an open or semi-open adoption. » (https://familienportal.de/familienportal/leben-slagen/kinderwunsch-adoption/adoption, last accessed August 21, 2019).

idyllic riverside and a community of women and children - which have apparently embraced Parvati and Suri in the meanwhile off-screen - the fleeting utopian moment briefly appears as a new possibility: to find a chosen family despite adverse conditions and to actually live unfettered by borders and boundaries. Finally Robert visibly feels true kinship for Suri - an emotion which is founded on their shared experiences in India rather than their shared genetic makeup - and as her uncle he wishes to be actively involved in her welfare without doubting any longer that Parvati is her mother and should raise her in India.

Images 6 and 7: Screenshots from the film *River of Life - Born on the Banks of Ganges*

Even though the final scene could indeed be read 'against the grain' in this very fashion, a close inspection reveals that the film does not really seem intent to pluralise that which, from the standpoint of the majority of German society, is yet thought of, sought after, and accepted as family. Because, even though Paravati's name points to the Hindu mother-goddess, the character - as well as the resolution to the central question and conflict of where a child procreated by means of assisted reproductive technologies, and then not collected by the commissioning mother, truly belongs - rather clearly conforms to a normative image of mother- and womanhood as characterised by common conceptions, discussions and legal definitions in Germany to this very day. One scene in particular illustrates how the film primarily reproduces and, as it were, 'outsources' the continually dominant normative understanding of the unity of biological and social mother- and parenthood. After Robert succumbs to the strains of the search for Suri, he wakes up in hospital with Jörg Lewanski, an employee of the German Embassy, already at his bedside who quickly briefs him on the alleged legal situation in India: »Singles cannot commission a surrogate any longer« (1:18:20 h). Robert's objection that this had not been the case two years prior is met with a statement crucial for German television viewers: the embassy official explains, to an apparently ignorant Robert, that according to Indian law whoever gives birth to a child is considered his or her legal mother. Precisely this principle, to under no circumstances permit a splitting of motherhood, is central to the German Embryo Protection Act of 1991, however. This legislation justifies the strict ban on surrogacy, whether commercial or altruistic, as well as the ban on egg donation. That fatherhood on the other hand is considered divisible in the eyes of the German legislator is apparent in the approval of sperm donation.

A Glimpse Into the Current Debate in Germany

Although this strict ban apparently still meets with majoritarian approval, there have been occasional critical articulations. For instance, organisations such as the German Bar Association (DAV) or the Federal Association of German Registrars (BDS) have demanded »Germany to face reality«: »Surrogacy may be banned in Germany. But globalisation has already made it part of our lives«, read a press release by the German Bar Association from August 11th, 2014.[47] This official recognition and the realisation that the feasibilities of reproduction technologies, of course, also lead German citizens to increasingly make use of the legal grey-areas and offers of transnational reproduction tourism in order to have genetic children, has long been taboo in Germany. In public discussions, on talk shows, as well as with regard to heavily mediatised individual cases, intended parents are conspicuously often pathologised for their strong wish for a genetic child. Besides the question of how children are supposed to come into this world, the question of who is actually allowed to have access to the model of the middle-class nuclear family with genetic offspring has been of central importance in the current German debate. Singles, infertile or same-sex couples were thus far excluded from this model of family life - and ought to be in widely held opinion. They were expected to simply yield to, or rather accept, their 'fate' of childlessness. Simultaneously, also in Germany the societal pressure to have children prevails and especially heterosexual childless couples who wish for a child are almost inevitably faced with the ethical dilemma of having to decide how far they are willing to go for the realisation of that aspiration - not seldom with the people around them constantly referencing the 'feasibility' by means of assisted reproductive medicine. In this context, the talk of 'humanitarian' reasons which are to justify the access to surrogacy

---

47   The full version of the press release (in German) can be found online at: https://anwaltverein.de/de/newsroom/pm-23-14 (last accessed August 21, 2019).

for certain couples is particularly interesting. For instance, Jürgen Rast, president of the German Bar Association (DAV) and vice-president of the Federal Association of German Registrars (BDS) suggests: »If couples are unable to conceive, it is acceptable on humanitarian grounds to provide them with access to surrogacy [...]. If the principle of surrogacy, however, degenerates into a business practice, it is to be strictly rejected (dpa, 06.08.2014)«.[48] This rhetorical recourse to the language of 'humanitarianism' and 'human rights' also took place recently in the context of the discussion of the ban on commercial surrogacy in India - significantly employed by the internationally most visible representative of the Indian reproductive market, Dr. Nayana Patel from Anand, Gujarat. Patel repeatedly and very effectively raises the question across media platforms: »Why take away the basic human right to have a baby?« (see the previous chapter in this volume).[49]

Is a right to procreation really imaginable, and would that imply that, at least, those who are considered a family in a normative and legal sense have to be provided with access to reproductive medicine - if need be, state subsidised, so that it is also available to poor families? And who, then, will be regarded as family, still mostly heterosexual and married couples, or also same-sex couples[50] - and what about singles who do not have a partner but want children regardless? When same-sex couples, as well as singles, were barred from obtaining medical visas to India for the purpose of commissioning a surrogate in 2013,[51] the real intention behind the move - according

---

48   The full press release (in German) is available online at: http://www.t-online.de/leben/familie/schwangerschaft/id_70532928/leihmutterschaft-deutsche-standesbeamte-fordern-lockerung-des-verbots.html (last accessed August 21, 2019).

49   See for instance her interview with *The Guardian* (03/02/2016), available online at: https://www.theguardian.com/world/2016/jan/03/india-surrogate-embryo-ban-hardship-gujarat-fertility-clinic (last accessed August 21, 2019).

50   On December 19th 2014, the Federal Supreme Court, (Bundesgerichtshof, BGH) issued a landmark ruling that recognized for the first time German intended parents as the legal parents of a child born through surrogacy. The case involved a same-sex couple from Berlin whose child was born through a surrogate in California. While Intended Parents are still unable to legally pursue surrogacy in Germany, it was expected by some observers that the ruling might generate a more positive regard toward surrogacy and potentially encourage legislative changes. Opinions on this, however, continue to be deeply divided in Germany.

51   Since 2013 and until commercial surrogacy was banned in India, foreign nationals intending to visit India for the purpose of commissioning surrogacy had to apply for a medical visa which was subject, among other, to the condition that

to several assessments, also from India - was not only to dodge the already looming legal problems with countries that prohibit any form of surrogacy, but above all, to avoid the heteronormative image of family in India itself being subject to change.

Promoting 'Authentic Actors' - Authenticating the 'Documented Reality' in a Fictional Film

Pegah Ferydoni plays the character of Parvati as an ever active, energetic and reflective woman who does not want to accept that she, supposedly, cannot make something more out of her life. Parvati's desire for ICT-skills and a career to supply her with a regular income, independence from her husband, and the prospect of social mobility is an expression of that very attitude. The popular actor was born in Teheran in 1983 and fled the Iranian regime with her artistic and politically active parents to Germany, where she grew up and lives to this day with her family. Ferydoni is best known to German television viewers in her role of the devout Muslim daughter Yağmur in the successful TV series *Turkish for Beginners* (2006-2009), who has to come to terms with suddenly being a stepsister and -daughter in a German-Turkish patchwork family. It would be difficult not to relate her career as a German actor with the lively debate of the last years on the difficulties experienced particularly by non-white or immigrant actors to be cast, beyond the usual stereotypical and ethnicised roles, in German cinema or feature films. Besides the fact that, before *Born on the Banks of Ganges,* she had already played an Indian on previous TV productions, her being a (single) mother herself was possibly of significance for her being cast as Parvati. As the successful promotion and communication of lavishly produced motion pictures is decisively dependent on the creation and cross-media marketing of 'authenticity', actors, cast and staged as quasi-testimonial, are supposed to actively create and convey. This fluidisation between 'private life' and film roles presented for the sake of PR is surely not a novel

---

»(i) The foreign man and woman are duly married and the marriage should have sustained at least for two years.« Source: http://boi.gov.in/content/surrogacy (content no longer available, it is now stated on the same website that, »Vide Government of India guidelines dated 03.11.2015, the foreign nationals including OCI/PIO card holders are not allowed to commission surrogacy in India.« Last accessed August 13, 2019).

phenomenon, yet, its qualitative dimension has rapidly shifted with social media and social bots in particular. The individual decision to which extend this staging of 'public intimacy' is tolerable in each case can be crucial for an acting career.[52]

In contrast to Ferydoni's unwillingness to utilise her own motherhood for PR purposes, however, she apparently felt an acute need to impart information on India. Interestingly, the actor does not only refer to her experiences during or besides filming in Varanasi, but rather concretely to the numerous elements of a 'documented reality' which the film employs in many scenes depicting the city and river life. In the interviews she expresses near astonishment concerning the fact that the film kept quite a few of the scenes which Ferydoni describes as authentic of the 'reality of the city of Varanasi' using documentary film techniques, when she expected them to end up on the cutting floor of the displeased ZDF editors.[53] What Ferydoni paints as the reality, visualised and documented in the film, is however primarily what she, as a European, experienced as challenging, or rather at times overcharging, as she states in the interview. These are without exception central topoi in the visual and textual representation of India, as they are known from uncounted coverages, travel accounts and documentaries: a sense of chaos, dirt and visible poverty attached to the impression of too many people at one place - that is, the topos of overpopulation. In the course of the promotion of the film, the actor has repeatedly alluded to these topoi in rather drastic imagery during individual interviews and on talk shows with considerable numbers of spectators.[54]

In the film itself the supposedly 'confusing and chaotic state' of India's reproductive market is explained by two characters: firstly by Dr. Rohini, as already cited above, and secondly by a member of the German embassy in Delhi, Jörg Lewanski. From Parvati, the surrogate, herself we hear little

---

52 An interview with Ferydoni which was published under the headline »She Speaks Openly About Her Child for the Very First Time« shortly before the film's premiere in Germany's most successful celebrity news magazine BUNTE, is especially instructive in this regard. BUNTE, The full interview was published on the day of the film premiere at: https://www.bunte.de/entertainment/film/tuerkisch-fuer-anfaenger-star-pegah-ferydoni-sie-spricht-erstmals-offen-ueber-ihr-kind.html (last accessed August 13, 2019).

53 See for instance her interview with Christian Behring in the course of the ZDF press day in promotion of the television film on January 27, 2007. Online available at http://www.redcarpetreports.de/2017/news/pegah-ferydoni-und-heinz-hoenig-im-herzkino-wir-sprachen-mit-ihnen/ (last accessed August 13, 2019).

54 For instance also in the popular talk show *Markus Lanz* from February 1st, 2017.

less than a hint at her perspective on this physically and emotionally challenging labour. The visualisation of her living conditions, however, are
worth mentioning since these sequences were, as Ferydoni emphasises, »in
fact shot in a real slum« (ibid.). The televisualization of extreme poverty
and the surrogate mother's life in a slum was done in strikingly similar way
in the first feature film about surrogacy and reproductive tourism to India,
Monsoon Baby (2014) which will be introduced in the following section.

Repro-Dramas as a Way of Translating Expertise Across Different Domains of Knowledge?

The film *Monsoon Baby* was produced for the other big broadcasting channel in Germany, ARD and was first screened in mid-September 2014 and
for the second time in August 2016, achieving a television audience of more
than 5 million viewers. In addition to that, a number of long articles about
the film were published in the big daily newspapers and news magazines
and many more reviews could be found online. This surely had to do with
the 'sensational' topic, as it was the first fictional drama which focused on
reproductive tourism from Germany to Asia, and on surrogacy in India, but
also with the fact that the director, Andreas Kleinert, is well-established and
enjoys a good reputation for 'high quality' television dramas; he is also a
faculty member at the renowned Filmuniversität Babelsberg Konrad Wolf
in Potsdam.

The story is about a young married couple, Nina and Mark, who for many
years have 'tried everything' in order to have their own genetic child. After
having invested much more than what they earn (Nina works as a nurse in
a birth clinic, while Mark runs a small carpentry) in legally available, but
rather costly IVF treatments in Germany, they feel that a surrogate mother
in India would be the only remaining 'last resort' for them. In a fertility clinic
in Kolkata, they select Shanti as their surrogate and the fertilized egg cell is
accordingly implanted in Shanti's uterus, using Nina's and Mark's own gametes. Upon her return to Germany, however, Nina realizes how difficult it
is for her to keep pretending for weeks and months that a baby is growing
in her belly, as the couple finds it extremely difficult to talk to their family
and friends about the split motherhood and commissioned surrogacy arrangement in India. When Nina finally reveals the truth to a friend and colleague who harshly criticizes her for being so selfish and not thinking about
how she and her husband are adding to the exploitation of an extremely poor
woman in India, both sides seem to be well-informed about the intricacies

and highgly exploitative structures of a globalized reproductive market. The ethical dilemma and everyday practical problems that the intended parents are faced with become increasingly hard to navigate, especially for Nina. She also realizes how difficult it is to feel a sense of kinship when the pregnancy and growth of 'her' child is technologically mediated and cannot be experienced through a physical co-presence. Very clearly, the anxiety of not being able to 'control' the surrogate mother Shanti adds to Nina's stress. She decides to go back to Kolkata and help out in Kamalika's clinic which is visually represented as a run-down place with almost no personnel, so that Nina's voluntary service work is highly welcomed by the director and doctor in charge. Shanti, in the meantime, has disappeared without a trace, persecuted - once again - by a very violent husband who was apparently not at all aware of the surrogacy. Mark arrives in Kolkata and together with Nina and Kamalika, they begin the search for the meanwhile heavily pregnant Shanti in the wetlands.

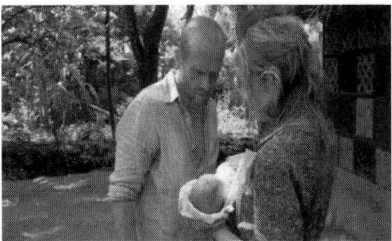 

Images 10 and 11: Stills from the film *Monsoon Baby* (DVD, 2014), showing Nina and Mark holding and looking in disbelief at 'their long desired genetic child'.

When they finally find her in what seems to be her birthplace, Shanti is very ill and after an emergency C-section which is conducted in her hut, the baby is alive and well, but it remains open whether the ailing surrogate mother will survive or not. It also remains open whether Nina and Mark will be able to bring 'their' child 'home', as the film ends with a rigid staff member of the German embassy who makes it very clear to them that he is not willing to issue a German passport for the baby and does not believe that Nina has really given birth to the child in India.

The fact that one of the co-writers of the screenplay for this film is Florian Hanig, a trained journalist and successful author of scripts on topical issues which require a lot of research and contextual knowledge, sets *Monsoon Baby* apart from many other television dramas. Before developing the idea for the script, Hanig had already researched on commercial surrogacy in South Africa and written a long-term reportage about a commissiong couple from Germany. While working on another story about the school system in India, as he describes in an interview, he accidentally came across a fertility clinic and was instantly able to talk to the clinic personnel and also to some of the surrogate mothers about their motivation for this work and their personal aspirations. An image which he found particularly unsettling during his visit in the clinic was the moment when he saw how

»a light-skinned baby was pulled out of the belly of a dark-skinned woman in a Sari. Instead of putting the child to her breast, the newborn baby was immediately handed

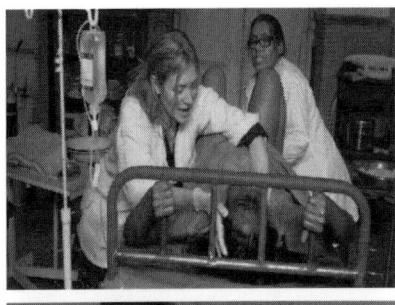

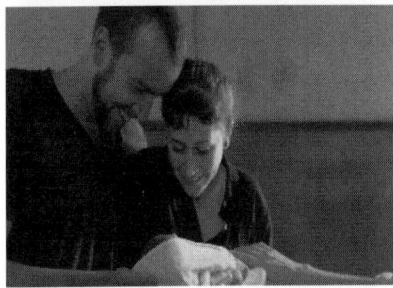

Images 12-16: Stills from the film Monsoon Baby (DVD, 2014).

over to the European couple which was waiting in front of the surgery room. While the Indian woman just turned her head to the side, her body shaking with cramps«.[55]

Asked by the journalist if *Monsoon Baby* could thus be considered an 'authentic' film, Hanig replied, »yes, even if the story is fictitious« (ibid.).

As mentioned in the previous chapter in this volume, the camera's gaze as well as the viewer's gaze on the laboring bodies of surrogate mothers during childbirth is an ethically questionable and yet rarely discussed aspect in a number of documentary films about reproductive tourism and commercial surrogacy in India. While the corresponding visualization of the scene in *Monsoon Baby*, which is so vividly described by Hanig, thus clearly draws on these already established forms of a 'documented reality', in this feature film, the camera moves even much closer to the laboring body and especially to the face of the surrogate mother immediately after the child has been handed over to the waiting couple behind the curtain, her face covered with sweat and tears. The surrogate does not speak, neither the one we see in the scene below nor Shanti, the surrogate mother who agreed to carry Nina's and Mark's child and who has only very few dialogues in the whole film. It is, once again, the doctor in charge who speaks for her and other 'observing experts' who interpret and comment on the situation. In this remarkable and deeply ambiguous scene in the film, while we see others gazing from different distances and perspectives onto the laboring body of the surrogate mother who never looks or speaks back, clearly we are invited to question the postionality of our own gaze.

Despite an abundance of very essentializing representations and stereotypical visualizations in this film too, *Monsoon Baby* obviously makes an effort to 'translate' and communicate knowledge to its audience and the dialogues invite viewers time and again to raise questions about the repercussions of split mother- and parenthood - about the ethical and moral dilemmas of what is technologically feasible and increasingly on demand, the many legal problems as well as the unpredictable risks and potential consequences, primarily for the surrogate mother but also for thecommissioning parents. Contrary to *River of Life - Born on the Banks of Ganges*, however, *Monsoon Baby* visualizes the emotional and physical labor but fails to show

---

55   The interview (German original version) is available online at: http://www.br.de/presse/inhalt/pressedossiers/monsoon-baby-interview-florian-hanig-100.html (last accessed August 21, 2019). Hanig also mentions in the interview that he has a special relationship to the country: his wife is from Bombay and they have two sons.

the voice and agency of surrogate mothers who are mostly shown as powerless victims of poverty and patriarchal violence. It is also problematic that both films never question the power relation between the fertility clinic, the doctors in charge and the surrogates. Especially in *Monsoon Baby*, the clinic is represented as a welcome break from the surrogates' gruesome every day and marital life, almost like a 'holiday' which allows them to have a social life, chat with other surrogate mothers, drink tea and where they receive much better healthcare than most other women in India. The deeply problematic aspect of constant surveillance of medicalized bodies in the surrogacy hostels, and of the disciplinary project of transforming 'surrogates' into 'perfect-mother workers', as Amrita Pande calls it, is never touched upon and in the end, it is the 'compassionate' and 'righteous physician' (an iconic and ubiquitous figure in German television entertainment), Kamalika, who personally searches for Shanti and saves the child for the German couple, and possibly the ailing surrogate too.

Conclusion

While reproductive tourism and the surrogacy market in India is a transnational phenomenon, the visibility, knowledge transfer and generation of an 'informed' critical debate in a context like Germany still largely depends on the structures and dynamics of a national media system. The chapter focussed not only on the form and content of two lavish productions which were successfully screened on the two biggest public-service broadcasting channels, ARD and ZDF, between 2014 and 2017, but more specifically on the ways in which the central theme was communicated and reflected upon across different media and platforms. By doing so, it described how different communicative practices, actors, media and techniques were involved or combined to create a general impression that despite being feature films based on fictitious stories, both films had observational or documentary sequences which made them communicable as 'authentic' and that both productions had been motivated by an urgent matter of importance. However, by problematising the prevalent visual reproduction of essentialized and Eurocentric fears of an 'opaque' and 'uncontrollable' Orient, the chapter finally argues that while the two dramas may indeed have succeeded in communicating 'findings' and 'knowledge' about the social repercussions of technological innovations in the field of Assisted Reproductive Technologies to very different audiences, precisely the potential for German society to 'interrogate itself' seems to be rather limited.

References

Films

Monsoon Baby (2014), directed by Andreas Kleinert.
River of Life - Born on the Banks of Ganges (2017), directed by Michael Karen.

Literature

Behring, Christian (2016). »Pegah Ferydoni und Heinz Hoernig im Herzkino – Wir sprachen mit ihnen«. *RedCarpet Reports*, 29 Jan 2016. https://www.redcarpetreports.de/2017/news/pegah-ferydoni-und-heinz-hoenig-im-herzkino-wir-sprachen-mit-ihnen/ (last accessed August 21, 2019).

BR (2014). »Monsoon Baby, Drehbuchautor Florian Hanig«. 16 Jul 2014. https://www.br.de/presse/inhalt/pressedossiers/monsoon-baby-interview-florian-hanig-100.html (last accessed August 21, 2019).

Bundesministerium für Familie, Senioren, Frauen und Jugend. »Welche Formen der Adoption gibt es?« https://familienportal.de/familienportal/lebenslagen/kinderwunsch-adoption/adoption (last accessed August 21, 2019).

Chaudhuri, Maitrayee (2015). »National and Global Media Discourse after the Savage Death of 'Nirbhaya': Instant Access and Unequal Knowledge«. In: Schneider, Nadja-Christina and Titzmann, Fritzi-Marie (Eds.). *Studying Youth, Media and Gender in Post-Liberalisation India. Focus on and Beyond the 'Delhi Gang Rape'*. Berlin: Frank & Timme, Reihe: Kommunikationswissenschaft, Band 6. 19-44.

Deomampo, Daisy (2016). *Transnational Reproduction. Race, Kinship, and Commercial Surrogacy in India*. New York University Press.

Deutscher Anwaltverein (2014). »Pressemitteilung Rechtspolitik. Leihmutterschaft: Deutschland braucht eine gesetzliche Regelung, um sich der Realität zu stellen«. Aug 11, 2014. https://anwaltverein.de/de/newsroom/pm-23-14 (last accessed August 21, 2019).

Deutsche Presseagentur (2014). »Unerfüllter Kinderwunsch. Deutschlands oberster Standesbeamter fordert Legalisierung von Leihmutterschaft«. Aug 06, 2014. https://www.t-online.de/leben/familie/schwangerschaft/id_70532928/leihmutter-schaft-deutsche-standesbeamte-fordern-lockerung-des-verbots.html (last accessed August 21, 2019).

Doshi, Vidhi (2016): »'We Pray that this Clinic Stays Open': India's Surrogates Fear Hardship from Embryo Ban«. *The Guardian*, Jan, 3 2016. https://www.theguardian.com/world/2016/jan/03/india-surrogate-embryo-ban-hardship-gujarat-fertility-clinic (last accessed August, 21 2019).

Gupta, Jyotsna Agnihotri (2012). »Reproductive Biocrossings: Indian Egg Donors and Surrogates in the Globalized Fertility Market«. *International Journal of Feminist Approaches to Bioethics* 5(1): 25-51.

Hepp, Andreas (2013). *The Communicative Figurations of Mediatized Worlds: Mediatization Research in Times of the 'Mediation of Everything'*, 2013. Published online at: https://www.kommunikative-figurationen.de/fileadmin/user_upload/Arbeitspapiere/CoFi_EWP_No-1_Hepp.pdf (last accessed August 21, 2019).

Hochschild, Arlie Russell (2012). *Outsourced Self: Intimate Life in Market Times.* New York: Metropolitan Books.

Inhorn, Marcia (2015). *Cosmopolitan Conceptions: IVF Sojourns in Global Dubai.* Durham: Duke University Press.

Knecht, Michi; Klotz, Maren and Stefan Beck (eds.) (2012). *Reproductive Technologies as a Global Form. Ethnographies of Knowledge, Practices, and Transnational Encounters.* Frankfurt am Main: Campus.

Koch, Florian (2017). »'Türkisch für Anfänger'-Star Pegah Ferydoni: Sie spricht erstmals offen über ihr Kind«. *BUNTE*, Feb 5, 2017, https://www.bunte.de/entertainment/film/tuerkisch-fuer-anfaenger-star-pegah-ferydoni-sie-spricht-erstmals-offen-ueber-ihr-kind.html (last accessed August 21, 2019).

Majumdar, Anandita (2013). »Nurturing an Alien Pregnancy: Surrogate Mothers, Intended Parents and Disembodied Relationships«. *Indian Journal of Gender Studies* 21(2): 199-224.

---. (2014). »The Rhetoric of the Womb: The Representation of Surrogacy in the Popular Mass Media in India«. In: DasGupta, Sayantani and DasGupta, Shamita Das (eds.). *Globalization and Transnational Surrogacy in India: Outsourcing Life.* Lanham: Lexington. 106-123.

Mitra, Sayani and Hansen, Solveig. »Auf der anderen Seite der Kamera. Leihmutterschaft in Indien und das moralische Anliegen der Dokumentarfilmerin Surabhi Sharma«. *Ethik der Medizin* 27(1): 69-80.

Pande, Amrita (2014). *Wombs in Labor: Transnational Commercial Surrogacy in India.* New York: Columbia University Press.Schneider, Nadja-Christina and Titzmann, Fritzi-Marie (2014). *Studying Youth, Media and Gender in Post-Liberalization India: Focus on Sexual Violence, New (Im)Mobilities and Evolving Gender Identities.* Berlin: Frank & Timme, Reihe: Kommunikationswissenschaft, Band 6.

Strathern, Marilyn (2002). »Still Giving Nature a Helping Hand? Surrogacy. A Debate about Technology and Society«. *Journal of Molecular Biology* 319(4): 985-993.

Vora, Kalindi (2009). »Indian Transnational Surrogacy and the Commodification of Vital Energy« *Subjectivities* 28(1): 266-278.

Chapter 4: An Absent or Present Family? Tracing Bollywood Films from the Turn of the Century

Parul Bhandari

Indian cinema, particularly Bollywood, has depicted the Indian family in diverse facets.[56] Indeed, the family has been the main trope for Indian cinema, extending across genres — Drama, comedy, political satires, Horror, Crime, Thriller, and web-series (Netflix, Amazon Prime). For example, often in the crime-genre, the criminal-gang or "organisation" is set-up around a family, or the protagonist's inclination to criminal activities is explained as emanating from a trauma of being from a broken family. In the horror genre, unfulfilled desires of a family member or their mistreatment is often shown as the cause of haunting. Web-series too, have used the prism of the family to depict and discuss social and political dystopias, such as Leila (Netflix), that showcases the perils of a totalitarian regime through the lens of a mother-daughter relationship. In this chapter, I focus on the Drama/Comedy/Romance genre of Bollywood, to examine if there has been any shift in the way the family is depicted in recent films.

This theme of enquiry will not only help to establish a chronological order of Bollywood films but will also allow to trace broader societal changes in India. This is because often Bollywood films serve as a navigating tool to understand the society's mood — cultural, political, religious. For example, films made in post-independence years, mainly discussed themes of nation-building and aspirations related to that, such as, the end of corruption, socialist ideologies, the evils of feudalism. A popular way to capture these nation-building goals was by humanising the nation as a family member who struggles and finally overcomes difficulties, thereby also putting into focus the essential place of family in the making of the Indian nation. One such example is of *Mother India* (1957), where the mother fends for her children, fighting the corrupt agricultural lending-system. Another pop-

---

56   I use the term Bollywood in its expansive definition, implying Hindi cinema. For further discussion on what Bollywood means for India, and if indeed Bollywood can be seen as a genre in itself, see Dwyer (2011), Kaur and Sinha (2005).

ular theme was to capture the changing dynamics related to land by depicting how property can be a point of dispute between family members and therefore, a 'new' India needs better laws. Another set of films depicted the changing village-kinship dynamics, as one member leaves for the city for employment, and in this way captured the benefits and also challenges of migration. As Indian society progressed, the family faced new challenges, for example, there emerged a wave of feminism, which questioned patriarchal traditions of dowry, treatment meted out to daughters-in-law, assertion of choice in marriage, and explored tabooed topics of sexualities (*Fire* 1996).[57] Each of these films, thus, were chronicles of the changes that India was witnessing, and in this chapter, I will pick up from where scholarship left last — the 1990's, which is the era when Indian family's most unified face was depicted, through NRI families or films which appealed to NRI audiences (Desai 2007; Jaikumar 2006; Kaur and Sinha 2005). I will thus analyse, if since the 2000's the family is depicted any differently, and if so, how this depiction resonates with contemporary Indian family dynamics?

This is indeed an interesting line of enquiry for the 2000's have ushered swift changes in Indian society with the widespread use of technology (mobile phones to smartphones; internet), the 'opening' of Indian economy, a bourgeoning leisure and consumption culture (malls, international brands, pubs, wining and dining culture), the increasing acceptance of diverse sexual identities and pre-marital relationships, and the delay of marriage (especially in urban areas). The question then is whether the films made since the 2000's capture any of these changes or their essence by depicting the family any differently? In order to address this question, I put forth my analysis in three sections: firstly, I provide a brief chronology of the ways in which the family has been depicted in Bollywood until the 1990's, and argue that the two broad themes that dominate the films of the 2000's and 2010's (also referred to as 'new Bollywood' or 'recent films' in this chapter), are the absent family and the bickering family. In the next section, I analyse the theme of the absent family, as I discuss how recent love stories, relegate the family to the background, and I explain how this is related to the 'new' middle class identities. In the third section, I turn attention to the theme of the bickering family by providing an in-depth analysis of the 2016 film, *Kapoor & Sons* (*KS*), which, I argue, leads the trend of depicting interfamily dynamics with nuance. With these discussions I infer that recent Bollywood films depicted the family differently as they do not show the family in its

---

57   For further discussion on the making and reception of *Fire* (1996), see Ghosh (2010).

united or exalted avatar but instead capture the contesting, conflicting inter-family dynamics, shaped by individual members' unique struggles, aspirations, and desires, which resonates with the contemporary urban middle's sensibilities and sense of 'self' worth and self-assessment.

1. *Depiction of Family until the 1990's*

Scholarship has ascertained a chronology of the themes that Bollywood has addressed in successive years (Desai 2007; Kaur and Sinha 2005). While these categorisations are certainly helpful, the family is not their central theme of analysis. Addressing this gap, I propose another categorisation of Bollywood films on how they have depicted changes in Indian society through the prism of the family. This categorisation is not strictly chronological, though it is possible that one theme is dominant in specific times.

1.1 Struggles for the Family

Films that were made immediately after independence often focussed on communicating those goals and ideals that were essential for nation-building such as poverty alleviation, better bureaucracy, fighting feudalism, and so on. In these story plots, the focus was not so much on the family, rather, on the individual whose struggles of making ends meet, of raising a family, or fighting a system (of mortgage, bureaucracy, or feudalism) was the prism through which the desired ideals of a new Indian nation were communicated.

In an offshoot of this theme, the family did make an appearance, especially in the films of 1970's and 1980's, when the central character was either an abandoned child or an orphan, yearning for love and recognition from his family, or when the protagonist was shown to battle several problems to provide for his family (interestingly, the protagonist in these films is always male). Some of these films include *Muqaddar ka Sikander* (Conqueror of Destiny, 1978), *Trishul* (Trident, 1978), *Laawaris* (Orphan, 1981), *Coolie* (1983). Though the central theme of these films was to depict those characteristics that are desirable for the making of a 'new' India, the family made an appearance as that institution which provides emotional and moral support to the struggling protagonist. In other words, these films conveyed that the family will remain a resilient social system even for a new Indian identity. In this way, we were presented with an awe-inspiring, chaste, unity-providing image of the family. This was an important theme for after a long independence struggle, the Indian population needed to be inspired and reminded of the greatness of an Indian identity, and these films conveyed to the audiences that so long as they have the support of their family, they can overcome any struggles, and that if the Indian family could survive colonial rule, it could very well face other post-independence challenges.

1.2 The Family as a Site of Patriarchy

From eulogising the family, Bollywood turned attention to the problems in the institution of the family, as increasingly films began to highlight the family as a site of abuse, violence, and transgressions. The plot of these films essentially showcased how the 'safe place' (Sen 2016) of one's home and family can also be a breeding ground for abuse, as these stories captured the mistreatment of wives and daughters-in-law, for example in *Biwi Ho to Aisi* (The Ideal Wife, 1986) and *Daman* (Subjugation, 2001). Another set of movies traced the journey of inter-class and inter-religious couples whose families disapproved of their relationship, at times leading to their murder, such as in *Qayamat Se Qayamat Tak* (From Dooms Day till Dooms Day,1988) and *Bombay* (1995). In some ways, this shift in the depiction of a supporting family to an abusive one, was resonant with the changes that were taking place in India at large, where the next step of nation-building was to improve its social structures of gender, caste and family. It was around this time that there was a focus on controlling India's population (Sanjay Gandhi's infamous initiative of sterilisation in 1976), promoting inclusive growth (gender and caste), and a rise of social movements for greater representation and positive discrimination for the so-called lower castes. Indeed, the scene of Indian politics undergoes a transformative shift during this time with the formation of the Janata Party (on 23rd January 1977) (Guha 2007). Given these social and political changes, Bollywood films too adopted a critical gaze on the sacrosanct institution of the Indian family, laying bare its evils, and how these needed to be expunged for the family to continue being a beacon of support to the Indian population.

1.3 Re-integration of the Family

After this brief period of introspection, around the 1990's, the family re-emerged as the face of Indian cultural unity, this time, with the target audience of those Indians who were living abroad. These films primarily delineated the advantages of the Indian joint family system and were either on the Non-resident Indian population or catered to them. Desai (2007) argues that this was a 'revival' moment for Bollywood after the 'lost' decade of the 1980's (when films were mainly about sex and violence), as these films explained that its immigrant population is materially successful due to its Indian ethos and tradition, a big part of which is upholding one's family's honour and respecting family elders. [58]

This theme certainly resonated with the Indian society at that time, which had recently 'opened' its economy, and when there was heightened global movement of people, goods, images, and imaginations (Appadurai 1996; Ganguly-Scrase and Scrase 2009), as cities like Bangalore, Hyderabad, and Gurugram became centres of global India. Air travel became more accessible leading to frequent travel of NRIs to India, and technology and media (VCR, audio cassettes) allowed easy communication and outreach of Indian popular culture. In this context, movies on NRIs aimed for their re-integration to Indian society, by showing, for example, that despite living away from India, the NRIs hold on to Indian traditions and culture, such as a joint family, not speaking Hindi with an accent, and wearing Indian clothes at home and sometimes at work too. [59] A super-hit film that became synonymous to the conformist life of NRIs was *Dilwale Dulhaniya Le Jaayenge* (The Brave-hearted will take the Bride, 1995) (Uberoi 1998). This movie shows how the hero, Raj (Shah Rukh Khan) yearns to marry Simran (Kajol), the 'good Indian girl', but Simran's father (Amrish Puri) wants her to marry a 'good Indian boy' and not an immigrant Indian who is sullied by the cultures of the West. The primary plot of this love story is the strategies undertaken by Raj and Simran to get their love accepted by Simran's family,

---

58   A second theme of these films was on how India needs to be protected from an attack from the outsider, the 'other' (Muslim terrorist, mainly from Pakistan). For further discussion on depiction of the Muslim as the 'other' see Khan (2011), Mubarki (2014) and Vazira (2002).

59   These NRI films were not so much about 'Indians coming home but that India never left them' (Sharpe 2005: 66). Sharpe further notes that to that extent these were different than other NRI films such as *My Beautiful Laundrette* (1985) and *Bend It Like Beckham* (2002) that were more about second generation Indians and the inter-generational strife about asserting and resisting 'Indianness' and gendered identities.

without challenging the family's authority as the couples refuses to elope and marry. The main moral of this film (and others following this theme) is that the family might not always agree with the individual but ultimately has the individual's best interest at heart and can be won over by patience and respect. No other anxieties and desires of the individual, unrelated to the family, make any appearance in these films.

The decade of the 2000's brings a critical shift in the depiction of the family. Instead of nationalistic discourses, or critical appraisals, or eulogising of the family especially as appeasement to the NRIs, the family is now depicted broadly in two ways: it is either absent in the 'new' love stories, which focus more on the interpersonal dynamics of a couple, or takes the centre stage but this time the focus is on the everyday fractured inter-family dynamics. These films do not discuss any 'meta' obstacles faced by the family, such as financial troubles or land disputes, rather they shift attention to the 'micro' tensions in the form of everyday bickering, clash of personalities and expectations, yet also show how family members identify with their family despite the differences and frictions.

2. The Absent Family

The decades of the 2000's and 2010's saw several love stories, wherein the family (or gaining their approval) is no longer the central plot of the film. Unlike previous films, these films trace an individual's journey of personal growth in the narratives of love, instead of focusing on whether and how the family accepts their choice of romantic partner/spouse. These include films such as *Love Aaj Kal* (Love Nowadays, 2009), *Band Baja Barat* (Band, Trumpet, Marriage Procession 2010), *Break ke Baad* (After the Break, 2010), *I Hate Luv Storys* (I hate love stories, 2010), *Delhi Belly* (2011), *Rockstar* (2011), *Cocktail* (2012), *Dear Zindagi* (Dear Life, 2016).[60]

---

60   The title of the film *I Hate Luv Storys* does not use the correct spellings of 'Love' and 'Stories'. Rather, these words are spelled like a short hand text message, perhaps to resonate with the Indian (and indeed global) youth's preferences of texting-language.

2.1 The 'Neoliberal' Middle Class

As mentioned in the previous section, Bollywood films to a certain extent are a reflection of contemporary society, and these new love stories too establish a link of commonality with the audiences. One way in which this is achieved is through the background or character setting, as it were, of the central protagonists. For example, unlike previous films, the main characters of these films are not employed in public sector but work in the private sector (multinational companies) or pursue a career in the creative field (advertisement, marketing, architects, writers). These characters are shown as self-made, cosmopolitan, ambitious, often living away from their family. Furthermore, perhaps to depict India's cosmopolitan cultures, several of these films are based in Mumbai, Delhi, or foreign cities such as London, San Francisco, and Sydney. Another sub-set of these films are those which are based in smaller cities (less cosmopolitan) such as Jaipur, Lucknow, Mathura, Bareilly, Allahabad (Prayagraj) as shown in *Shudh Desi Romance* (Pure Local-styled Romance, 2013), *Shaadi mein Zaroor Aana* (Do Attend the Wedding, 2017), *Bareilly ki Barfi* (The Candy of Bareilly 2017), *Masaan* (Fly Away Solo 2017) *Luka Chuppi* (Hide and Seek, 2019), yet, these films too communicate a 'new' middle class identity through the professional ambitions of the main characters.[61] These protagonists too, for example, are shown as desiring greater independence from the family in matters of love, and are fiercely ambitious who do not want to carry on with their family business (clothes or sweet shop), and instead focus on developing a sense of 'self', particularly by following chosen paths of profession. According to recent scholarship these characteristics are indeed seen as the defining criteria of a 'new' middle class. This is to say, while the middle class of post-independent India focussed on achieving ideals that would help in nation-building, the 'new' (neoliberal) middle class has shifted its attention from the 'nation' to the 'self'. (Bhandari 2020; Deshpande 2003; Jodhka and Prakash 2016; Joshi 2011; Srivastava 1998, 2014). This is also evident in their everyday lives, as for example, Jodhka and Prakash (2016)

---

61   There is much contestation and scholarly debate on how the middle class can be defined – is it to be ascertained through economic criteria, or cultural or moral aspects, and is middle class a homogeneous category, or is it better to use the term 'middle classes' in order to denote the heterogeneity of this class. These themes of debates and discussions are pursued by works including Baviskar and Ray (2011), Bhandari (2020), Brosius (2010), Deshpande (2003), Dickey (2011), Donner (2011a), Fernandes (2006), Jaffrelot and van Deer (2008), Jodhka and Prakash (2016) and Sridhan (2011).

note that the 'new' middle class is increasingly concerned with their physical and psychological wellbeing as they are opting for regular health check-ups, therapy and counselling, gym memberships and fitness regimes.

These themes of focus on the 'self' then make way in these new Bollywood films where the central character is often shown as fragile, vulnerable or conflicted, trying to reconcile their professional dreams with desire of love (from others or self-love), for example. To elucidate this point, in this chapter, I take two films as points of reference: *Kapoor & Sons* (*KS* henceforth) (2016) and *Luka Chuppi* (*LC* henceforth) (2019). Whilst *KS* was a bigger hit than *LC*, they both were critically acclaimed — *KS* for its brilliant acting and adept screenplay that beautifully captured simmering conflicts within a family, and *LC* for tackling a bold topic with a dash of humour.

In *KS*, we meet two brothers Rahul Kapoor (Fawad Khan) and Arjun Kapoor (Sidharth Malhotra), both living in London, but estranged. Whilst Rahul's first novel was a success, he is shown to struggle with writing his second novel. Arjun too is an aspiring novelist, who is living under his elder brother's shadow of success, and feels demotivated for his debut novel was rejected by publishers. Their mother, Sunita (Ratna Pathak), who lives with her husband in their family house in Coonoor (hill station in South India) is a housewife who desires to start her own business (as a franchise for her sister's popular bakery business), and their father, Harsh (Rajat Kapoor), leaves a financially secure job at a bank to start his own business, which to his dismay, runs into losses. What is distinctive about the background of these characters is that unlike previous films on the family, the main characters are not struggling to get a job as such, or experiencing deep financial losses, nor are they 'locked down' by the ennui of a government job. Likewise, in *LC*, we meet Guddu (Kartik Aryan), who is a reporter in Mathura, in Uttar Pradesh, and aspires to be a successful reporter in a cosmopolitan city (Delhi, Mumbai). Rashmi (Kirti Sannon) is the daughter of an influential politician and upon graduation returns from Delhi to Mathura for an internship in a news channel. Thus, we meet two youngsters, who have high professional aspirations and indeed the woman (Rashmi) dares to step into the 'man's world' of media. Therefore, the central characters of these new films are shown as independent, ambitious, young middle-class individuals whose journeys of professional pursuits are not defined by meta-narratives of development, bureaucratic efficiency, or ideologies of 'right' or 'wrong', but shaped by a strong sense of developing their 'self'. In this way, these characters make a direct appeal of commonality with their neoliberal urban middle class audiences, who too are increasingly opting for private sector employment and are involved in various pursuits of the 'self' (leisure, spiritual, wellbeing) (Bhandari 2020).

2.2 Interpersonal Dynamics of Romance

Another way in which these films focus on the narratives of the 'self' is by unpacking the making and unmaking of romantic journeys. This is done by depicting the many confusions that a romantic relationship may cause, such as whether to accept a friend's proposal (*Aisha* 2010, *Ae Dil Hai Mushkil* Hard to Live Without You, 2016), or whether to act on a feeling of attraction towards a colleague or friend (*Jaane tu ... Ya Jaane na* You know .... Or You Don't Know, 2008, *Band Baja Baraat* 2010, *I Hate Luv Storys* 2010) or deliberations about breaking-up a relationship in pursuit of a career or education or other reasons (*Love Aaj Kal* 2009, *Break ke Baad* 2010, *Cocktail* 2012). The unfolding of romance in these films, does not pivot around getting a desired union accepted by the family, rather it delves into the realities, difficulties, apprehensions and struggles of the romantic relationship itself. These films also allude to other experiences of romance that were not openly depicted in previous romantic films such as casual sex (hook-ups, one-night stands), drinking cultures, and so on.[62] In this setting, and with this focus on the romantic couple's interpersonal dynamics, the family takes a backseat. This is evident in the fact that 'meeting the parents' is no longer the decisive scene of these films.[63] This scene now has a fleeting presence, whereas in previous films it was considered the 'moment of truth' when the family would either accept or reject the union. Instead, in the new Bollywood films, the family is shown to already approve the individual's romantic choice and the film instead focuses on the range of emotions that the couple experiences through their romantic journey, from attachment, attraction to suffering, pain, confusion, and infidelity (Bhandari 2017).

At the same time, this is not to say that the family is completely eliminated from these narratives, as at times, the parents are shown in conversation with the main characters, assuaging their anxieties about particular romantic prospects such as in *Jaane tu ... Ya Jaane na* (2008), we see that the

---

62   Indeed, several popular 'item' songs (Brara 2010) are set in the backdrop of a club (*Angrezi Beat Pe* in the film *Cocktail*, 2012) or house party with drinking games (*Kar Gayi Chull* in *KS*).

63   For further discussion on the ritual of 'meeting the parents' see Bhandari 2020 Chapter 3.

mother, Savitri Singh Rathore (Ratna Pathak) is largely non-interfering in her son Jai Singh Rathore's (Imran Khan) romantic life, except on a few critical moments, when she gives him helpful advices.[64] At other times, the parents are replaced by a parental figure, such as a trusted older friend or relative. For example, in *Love Aaj Kal*, Veer Singh (Rishi Kapoor), an older man who is a café owner, advices the lead-actor, Jai Vardhan Singh (Saif Ali Khan) on his romantic life. In this way, the family has a less conspicuous presence in these films yet also conveys that the 'new' middle class continues to be embedded in the family.

3. The Bickering Family

The second theme that has emerged in the films of the 2000's and 2010's is one that puts the family at the centre of the plot. These films depict the internal dynamics of the family by focusing on their everyday fractured, contested, entangled interactions. Some of these films include *Piku* (2015), *Kapoor & Sons* (2016), *Badhai Ho* (Congratulations, 2018).[65] This is in stark contrast to previous films on the family that tended to essentially revolve around a 'meta' issue, such as property dispute or disapproved love relationship. The recent films, on the other hand, depict a range of issues that may cause tensions in the family such as a member's professional trajectory (or lack thereof), sexuality, lifestyle choices (non-marriage), and by doing so explain that dissent and tensions within a family can be multiple, individualistic, and diffused. This yet again resonates with the contemporary Indian middle class who, as explained above, have turned their gaze to the 'self'. As such, these films too, in depicting the micro family dynamics, reveal much about the 'self' (individual struggles and burdens) as much as about the family.

Kapoor & Sons (KS), best captures these discords in a family, as it unravels the multiple clashes of personalities and emotions in a nuclear family.

---

64   I have elsewhere (Bhandari 2020) discussed this new avatar, as it were, of the family in detail, as I argue that the family has not withdrawn control or its importance has not drastically diminished in governing an individual's life. Rather, the family now devices new ways to interact with the individual such that it now has a dispersed influence, non-dominant presence and decentralized way of control, yet it ensures to make itself relevant in changing Indian social realities.

65   The beginning of this trend can be traced back to Mira Nair's films *Monsoon Wedding* (2001), a film about upper-middle-class India, which depicts sensitive topics of 'sexual frankness' and 'sexual abuse' by following the lives of members of a family (Sharpe 2005).

The setting of the film is that all family members come together after a long while when the grandfather (Rishi Kapoor) suffers a heart attack. As the story unfolds, we see how even in this dismal circumstance, the family members clash and quibble as they have pent-up anger and resentment towards each other, which is intensified by their own burdens and secrets — Rahul, though professionally successful is hiding his sexual identity from his family; Arjun is dejected as he feels like the lesser preferred of the two sons, whose professional and creative ambitions are not supported by his family; Harsh is battling with the failure of his business venture and a rocky married life as he indulges in extra marital relations with a former colleague; and Sunita is convinced that her husband is having an affair, and is overwhelmed by the emotional and physical labour of managing the household and the strained familial dynamics. This film then (as well as others following this theme) questions and unsettles our idea of a united and happy Indian family. It presents us these fractured family dynamics primarily along four axes:

3.1 The Mundane Setting of Discords

One of India's famous film directors is Sooraj R. Barjatya, who is known for making films that depict the unity of an Indian joint family (largely upper-caste Hindu), as the family survives big conflicts and feuds. These families are usually wealthy business families, living in large mansions. As a result, the scenes that depict family conflicts are either long soliloquies or dialogues delivered at the entrance of a palatial house or in front of all family members. In contrast, the recent films, such as *KS* shift attention to the regular and everyday aspects of family life by capturing conflict scenes against the backdrop of a mundane task such as when the family is dining together in their typically middle class dining room and when they are getting a plumbing job done.

Food, as a growing body of work on eating and preparing meals demonstrates (Banerjee-Dube 2018; Donner 2011a, 2011b), is interwoven with practices of inclusion, exclusion, power, and hierarchy. At one level, the act of dining, as also shown in a Barjatya film, *Hum Saath Saath Hain* (We Are All Together, 1999), the tag line of which is »A family that eats together, plays together, stays together«, is a marker of unity or togetherness of the family, and at another level, dining lays bare the inequalities and asymmetries of the family — who is sitting at the head of the table, who is served first, who is allowed to speak-up and so on. Shakun Batra (director of *KS*) demonstrates cinematic genius by introducing us to the Kapoor's fractured interfamily dynamics at their dining table. With this scene, Batra cleverly subverts the Barjatya tradition where a family bonds over a meal, as he uses this moment to expose the tensions of this seemingly 'regular' nuclear middle-class family. We see how the parents support their elder son's (Rahul) chosen path of being a writer, while the father (Harsh) dismisses the younger son (Arjun) when he reveals that he has left his job to also write a novel. Sunita however encourages Arjun to follow his dreams, and Rahul too offers to help, but Arjun does not respond to his brother's offer. This scene then sets the tenor of the film, as we are introduced to the angry and agitated relationships in the family.

In another scene, the family members' resentment towards each other surfaces in a setting of a mundane household chore: a plumbing job. Sunita is miffed with Harsh as he has not summoned a plumber to fix a leaking toilet. Harsh finally comes around to doing so, and whilst he is supervising the plumbing job, Sunita finds out that without her permission Harsh has used-up her savings to invest in his business, which has failed. The setting of this scene brings to the fore the everyday workings of a typical middle-class family, as it is set at the intersections of discussing savings, house upkeep, juxtaposed with lies and deceit. In other words, unlike Barjatya films, there is nothing grand or stupendous about the setting. Instead, their discords and relationships unfold whilst carrying on daily household chores. As the scene proceeds, both Rahul and Arjun get involved and end up shouting and throwing things at each other. Sunita has to momentarily abandon her feelings of shock and betrayal at her husband, and instead act as peacemaker between her sons. Harsh has a sense of guilt and shame, especially given that his secret was outed in front of his sons and a stranger (the plumber) and copes with it by getting angry at everyone in the room. In this way, Batra juxtaposes the emotional (lies) with the practical (plumbing), extraordinary (revelations of secrets) with the ordinary (a household chore), thereby drawing our attention to the fact that feuds and frictions in the family are not all about grand settings and imposing dialogues. Rather, the dark side of family relations are revealed in the most nondescript situations.

3.2 Fraternal Frictions

Fraternal discord is indeed a popular theme in Bollywood films, and whilst previously these discords were captured in dramatic surroundings and dialogues (the famous dialogue of *Deewar,* Wall, 1975, during a face-off between Vijay Verma {Amitabh Bachchan} and Ravi Verma {Shashi Kapoor}), the more recent films depict the resentment in more mundane and less dramatic ways, for example, as the choice of music is sombre and the setting more everyday. In this vein, *KS* does not showcase the fraternal discord in one 'mega' scene but depicts the simmering tension and anger between the two brothers throughout the film. For example, in the first scene we see that Arjun deliberately does not answer Rahul's phone calls, who is calling to inform him about their grandfather's heart attack. Then, Rahul offers a flight ticket to India but Arjun declines. At the airport, Arjun gives Rahul a reluctant hug. As the film progresses, it appears that their dynamic is improving but then Tia (Alia Bhatt) comes into the picture. Tia has a fleeting crush on Rahul, and on a drunken night kisses him, not realising that Rahul is gay. In the meantime, Arjun confides in Tia that he is resentful of his brother because he thinks that Rahul stole his book idea, as the story line of Rahul's book, which went on to be a huge success, is astonishingly similar to Arjun's first unpublished novel. Yet, he never confronted his brother. A few days later, Arjun invites Tia to his grandfather's birthday party, where Tia realises that Rahul is in fact Arjun's brother. Arjun sees Tia and Rahul talk and feels jealous, but later Rahul assures him that he is not into Tia and is happy in his romantic relationship (without revealing that he is gay). Arjun is relieved. As Tia and Arjun get close, she confesses to him that she kissed Rahul. Arjun is furious as he feels that his brother yet again has betrayed him (the first time by stealing his novel's idea) and gets into a physical brawl with Rahul. At this moment, Rahul comes out to his brother. Unlike previous films, this film does not portray one brother as 'good' and the other as 'bad'. In fact, it reveals that they both have their own sets of anxieties and insecurities that at times brings out the worst in them. Crucially, the fraternal discord is not due to dispute over property or difference in ideology, or abandonment of one brother by the other. Rather, it is caused due to secrets, lack of transparency, and miscommunications, and in this way, *KS* brings attention to the everyday realities of friction and feuds that mark a family.

3.3 The Deceiving and Protecting Mother

During the climax scene it is revealed that Rahul in fact did not steal Arjun's story idea. Arjun had shared his manuscript only with his mother, and at the same time, Rahul too sent his manuscript to Sunita for her feedback. Sunita felt that Rahul was struggling to write the novel and suggested edits to his manuscript based on Arjun's manuscript. Sunita never confessed this to either brother and inadvertently let Arjun build up anger and resentment against Rahul, while Rahul remained perplexed as to why his younger brother was estranged from him. Arjun is hurt, shocked and angry at his mother, and Sunita profusely apologises to him explaining that she helped Rahul not because she loves him more than Arjun but because she thought that Rahul needed a confidence boost.

In this way, Sunita strengthens her bond with one son, whilst deceiving the other. This is a very interesting and nuanced depiction of a mother-son bond, which especially for Punjabi kinship (Das 1993) is sacrosanct. Moreover, Bollywood often depicts any distrust between mother and son in the context of when they are not related by blood (stepmother for example, *Beta*, 1992). Rarely do Bollywood films explore themes of deceit and betrayal in a mother-son relationship, especially caused by the mother.

In the climax scene, we also see that an otherwise supporting mother, Sunita is hurt, angry and shocked when her son's sexual identity is finally revealed to her. She berates Rahul for having kept his 'secret life' from her. In this way, *KS* unsettles the sacrosanct relationship between mother-son as epitomised in previous movies such as *Mother India* (1957) or *Karan Arjun* (1995), as Batra highlights the vulnerabilities and anxieties of a mother, thereby not depicting her as infallible (a more popular trope in Bollywood). Here, we see the mother-figure as bringing the family together and also causing frictions, as a pacifier and also a cause of resentment and anger. In the climax scene, as she is processing new information of her one son's sexual identity, and pleading with the other to not abandon her, she is confronted with the tragic news that her husband died in a car accident, moments after he confesses to her that he was having an extra-marital affair. Sunita is raging with anger and also struck by grief, trying to make sense of her own feelings and her new reality, without her husband. In one of the first scenes of the film the grandfather expresses his desire to get a 'Happy Kapoor family' picture clicked with his two sons and their respective families. The closing scene shows that despite the fact that Sunita's suspicions regarding Harsh's affair were confirmed right before his death, she sets aside her anger and poses for this 'happy family picture' with a life-sized photograph of Harsh, thus communicating that though he cheated on her, a Kapoor family is incomplete without him. We are left with this shot, wondering whether Sunita will ever forgive Harsh, though it is amply clear that she has accepted Rahul's sexual identity. In this way, the figure of the mother is no longer the pristine and infallible one, and instead she is shown as a human being with feelings and emotions that are at times enabling and at other times damning.

3.4 Sex and Sexuality

Live-in relationships are in some ways an elusive yet enigmatic practice, that though are prevalent in contemporary Indian society are not really acknowledged, and certainly not accepted.[66] Nonetheless, recent films have begun to address this phenomenon, such as *Shudh Desi Romance* (2015) and *Luka Chuppi* (2019).[67] The more recent of the two, *LC*, takes a unique approach to depict live-in relationships, as this form of relationship is not shown as entirely transgressive for the couple does not openly challenge family authority but considers a live-in as an experiment of romance, the end result of which is marriage. The story line is that Rashmi and Guddu develop feelings for each other, and while Guddu immediately proposes for marriage, in an unconventional turn it is the woman, Rashmi, who suggests that they get to know each first by being in a live-in relationship. In this way, the film at the outset, establishes a 'progressive' tenor, as it were. Guddu is surprised at the suggestion, and their mutual friend cautions them that since they do not live in a 'big' city, it will be difficult for them to be in a live-in relationship as the society norms are stricter in smaller cities. They decide that when on a work trip to another city (Indore), they will pretend to be a married couple and in this way, try out a live-in relationship, but Rashmi's only condition is that she will not have sexual relationships with Guddu as she wants to keep that part of the relationship for after-marriage. To a certain extent, the condition of 'no-sex' is not an anomaly as even in my research (Bhandari 2020) I noted that some professional middle class were of the opinion that sex is only meaningful in the context of a

---

66 This is also evident in the the sparse scholarship that exists on this topic. See Agrawal (2012) and Titzmann (2017).

67 As I finalize writing this chapter, a new film *Shubh Mangal Zyaada Saavdhan* (Beware of This Marriage) is soon to be released (Feb 21 2020), which is on the tabooed and sensitive topic of gay romance and marriage. This film is on the attempts of a gay couple to get their relationship accepted by their families, but no in an entirely somber and serious tenor (like previous films on this topic, including KS) but with laughter and humour. In doing so, this film is as much about the family members and their negotiations and struggles with this relationship, as much as it is about normalization and acceptance of homosexual relationships.

'serious' relationship, that is, where there is real love amongst the couple.[68] *LC* thus, explains the merits of a live-in relationship at the same time communicating that this arrangement does not necessarily imply also having a sexual relationship. To that extent, a live-in relationship may be transgressive in one way but is conformist in other ways.

As the film unfolds, we see how due to a comedy of errors, Guddu's family 'catches' him and Rashmi, and believe that they are a married couple. Guddu and Rashmi do not correct this misconception, because their families frown upon live-in relationships and in fact Rashmi's father remarks that he is glad that his daughter eloped and married and did not enter a live-in relationship. In order to not offend their family sentiments by revealing that they were indeed in a live-in relationship, Guddu and Rashmi start living like a married couple (without having sex), and make unsuccessful attempts to actually get married. In this way, though *LC* addresses the practice of live-in relationships— its appeal, benefits, and problems — it shows that these relationships also have certain limits (no sexual relationships) and their end goal is to transform into marriage. It also shows how a practice (live-in relationship) that challenges family authority can also reinstate the family's authority (by seeking their approval), thereby highlighting the importance of the family in an individual's journey of romantic and self-exploration.[69] This depiction, in some ways resonates with contemporary middle class sensibilities where there is a heightened desire of self-expression, self-discovery, and exploring a more individualistic life, without necessarily questioning the place of the family in these pursuits. In other words, whilst the neoliberal middle class certainly has turned its gaze inwards to their 'self', they have not completely detached from the family.

Conclusion

Patricia Uberoi (1993) noted that two aspects in the study of family require further enquiry: firstly, the qualitative dimension of love, sex, marriage and family life and secondly, family as a site of violence and exploitation (pp 37). Adding to this perspective, in 2004, in her seminal essay 'The Family in India', she remarked that »sociologists need to confront the dysfunctional and pathological aspects of family life...« (pp 297), and that a broadening

---

68   This finding was also noted by Sirisena (2018) in her ethnography on university students in Colombo.

69   For further discussion on the role of family in romantic relationships see Bhandari (2017).

of the agenda for sociological studies of the Indian family also warrants an engagement with »new sources of data – literature, the arts, popular culture...« (*ibid*). Since Uberoi's writings, scholarship on the family in India has certainly brought attention to various pathologies of the family (sexual abuse, domestic violence), yet what slips through the gaps is the more everyday experiences of dysfunctionality, one that is not about downright violence and abuse but more banal yet sinister.

In this chapter, I have addressed both of Uberoi's remarks, by bringing attention to the everyday dysfunctional aspects of a family through the lens of analysing contemporary Bollywood films. I have explained that these films are distinct from previous films on families as the plot of disjuncture or discord is not based on grand critical events, as it were, of property dispute or disapproved romantic relationship. Rather, these films have attuned themselves to a 'neoliberal' middle class pulse, as it were, which essentially concerns with analysing 'self' and representations of self. As a result, the focus of these new films is to unpack the real and everyday workings of the family, with which the individual struggles (betrayals, secrets, manipulations) and also to highlight how despite these frictions the family manages to be together. Crucially, unlike the films of the 1990's, the films of the 2000's and 2010's are not eulogising the family or hailing its unity. Rather, they are addressing the constant tensions and conflicts in the family to show how the family is at once fractured and united. Another distinctive aspect of these films is that though their focus has shifted to the individual — their personal struggles and aspirations, the individual is not shown to be disembedded from the family. For example, the plots of these films often are about live-in relationships, casual dating (see chapter by Strulik in this volume), or the quest for autonomy or professional pursuit, yet, these quests are not detached from the family, as the individual constantly refers to their family and seeks them out (for approval or counselling). Significantly, though, these films, unlike the previous films, do not show the family as a grand-standing and an all-encompassing entity, instead it depicts the family as absent yet present, fractured yet united.

References

Agrawal, Anuja. 2012. "Law and 'Live-In' Relationships in India." *Economic and Political Weekly* 47(39): 50–56.

Appadurai, Arjun. 1996. *Modernity at Large: Cultural Dimensions of Globalization.* Minneapolis: University of Minnesota Press.

Banerjee-Dube, Ishita. 2018. "Modern Mixes: The Hybrid and the Authentic in Indian Cuisine." In *Exploring Indian Modernities: Ideas and Practices*, eds. Leila Choukroune and Parul Bhandari. New Delhi: Springer.

Bhandari, Parul. 2017. "Pre-Marital Relationships and the Family in Modern India." *South Asian Multidisciplinary Academic Journal* (16).

———. 2020. *Matchmaking in Middle Class India: Beyond Arranged And Love Marriage*. Singapore: Springer.

Brara, Rita. 2010. "The Item Number: Cinesexuality in Bollywood and Social Life." *Economic and Political Weekly* 45(23).

Brosius, Christiane. 2010. *India's Middle Class: New Forms of Urban Leisure, Consumption and Prosperity*. London and New York: Routledge Kegan and Paul.

Das, Veena. 1993. "Masks and Faces: An Essay on Punjabi Kinship." In *Family, Kinship and Marriage in India*, ed. Patricia Uberoi. New Delhi: Oxford University Press, 198–224.

Desai, Radhika. 2007. "Imagi-Nation: The Reconfiguration of National Identity in Bombay Cinema in the 1990's." In *Once Upon a Time in Bollywood*, eds. Gurbir Singh Jolly, Zenia B. Washwani, and Deborah Barretto. Toronto: Tsarbooks, 43–61.

Deshpande, Satish. 2003. *Contemporary India: A Sociological View*. New Delhi: Viking.

Donner, Henrike. 2011a. "Gendered Bodies, Domestic Work and Perfect Families: New Regimes of Gender and Food in Begali Middle-Class Lifestyles." In *Being Middle Class in India: A Way of Life*, eds. Henrike Donner and Geert de Neve. London and New York: Routledge.

———. 2011b. "New Vegetarianism: Food, Gender and Neo-Liberal Regimes in Bengali MIddle Class Families." *South Asia: Journal of South Asian Studies* XXXI(143–169).

Ganguly-Scrase, Ruchira, and Timothy Scrase. 2009. *Globalisation and the Middle Classes in India: The Social and Cultural Impace of Neoliberal Reforms*. London: Routledge.

Guha, Ram. 2007. *India After Gandhi*. London: MacMillan.

Jaikumar, Priya. 2006. *Cinema: At the End of Empire*. Durham: Duke University Press.

Jodhka, Surinder, and Aseem Prakash. 2016. *The Indian Middle Class*. New Delhi: Oxford University Press.

Joshi, Sanjay. 2011. "The Spectre of Comparisons: Studying the Middle Class of Colonial India." In *Elite and Everyman: The Cultural Politics of the Indian Middle Classes*, eds. Amita Baviskar and Raka Ray. New Delhi: Routledge, 83–107.

Kaur, Raminder, and Ajay Sinha. 2005. *Bollyworld: Popular Indian Cinema Through a Transnational Lens*. London, New York, Singapore: Sage.

Sen, Ritu. 2016. "Child Sexual ABuse: Unearthing the Quiet Corners of 'Home.'" In *Women, Media, and Violence*, eds. Vidya Jain and Rashmi Jain. Jaipur: Rawat Publications, 107–15.

Sharpe, Jenny. 2005. "Gender, Nation, Globalization." *Meridians: Feminism, Race, Transnationalism* 6(1): 58–81.

Srivastava, Sanjay. 1998. *Constructing Post-Colonial India: National Character and the Doon School*. New Delhi: Taylor and Francis, Routledge.

———. 2014. *Entangled Urbanism: Slum, Gated Community and Shopping Mall in Delhi and Gurgaon*. New Delhi: Oxford University Press.

Titzmann, Fritzi-Marie. 2017. "Contesting the Norm? Live-in Relationships in Indian Media Discourses." *South Asia Multidisciplinary Academic Journal* (16). https://samaj.revues.org/4371.

Uberoi, Paticia. 2006. "The Family in India." In The Oxford India Companion to Sociology and Social Anthropology Vol 2, ed. Veena Das. New Delhi: Oxford University Press, 275–307.

———. 1998. "The Diaspora Comes Home: DIsciplining Desire in DDLJ." *Contributions to Indian Sociology* 32(3): 305–35.

———. 1993. *Family, Kinship and Marriage in India*. New Delhi: Oxford University Press.

Chapter 5: The Ambivalences of Negotiating Plural Affiliations. Muslim Middle Class and Dating in Lucknow

Stefanie Strulik

With liberalisation since the 1990s and greater mobility due to work, but also due to longer educational biographies, opportunities to socialize other than with relatives and outside immediate neighbourhoods have increased over the last 30 years in India. Moreover, the time span available prior to marriage has increased due to a rise in marriage age for urban middle class families (Bhandari 2017). This chapter will look at heterosexual premarital relations in North India in the context of these changes. The ethnographic material discussed originates from 18 months of ethnographic multi-sited fieldwork (Marcus 1989) between 2012 and 2016 in the city of Lucknow. [70] By looking at premarital relations of young middle class adults it is examined how (heteronormative) ideas about masculinity, femininity, middleclassness, (global) youth culture(s) and Indian modernity are negotiated in everyday life and how frictions with family or religious expectations are creatively solved. Particular attention is given to the new dating opportunities and the creation of new intimate spaces due to technological change. Subsequently the chapter focusses on how dating is perceived as embodied middleclassness and how this relates to the construct of »being modern«. The chapter concludes with some observations regarding the ways in which premarital relations offer possibilities to create, experience and act out plural forms of belonging.

---

70   Lucknow is the 8th biggest city in India and capital of the Northern state Uttar Pradesh. According to the latest Census, 26.36% of the approx. 5 Million inhabitants are Muslims (Govt. India 2011).

Stefanie Strulik

Why Muslim Middle Class?

According to governmental socio-economic criteria, the number of middle class households in India increased six-fold since the beginning of economic liberalization in 1993 (Krishnan and Hatekar 2017). In political and media discourse in India, »middle class« gets presented as the derivate of modernity and Indianness (Chacko 2018). This politicized narrative opens up new possibilities of constructing subjectivities that allow for (re)presenting oneself as Indian and »modern« at the same time. Middle class, hence, is not only a mere descriptive category of analysis, but also a contentious political project. Thereby the lower boundaries of middle class as a »category of practice«, (Bruebaker and Cooper 2000: 4) coincide with the differentiation between traditional/poor/backward and socially upward mobile, modern India. Despite the fact that about 90 Mio. Muslims could be categorized as belonging to the middle class (Krishnan and Hatekar 2017), Muslims usually do not feature in Indian narratives of the »rising middle class« and Indian modernity.[71] Moreover, in public discourse, Muslims tend to be represented as a 'problem', as »antinational« (Hasan 2008), »backward« (Amin 2005) or even »frozen in the past« (Hasnain 2009). The research project »*Muslim Middle Class and Competing Narratives of Modernity*«[72], from which the data discussed in this chapter is drawn, had the aim to make visible marginalized narratives of modernity and middleclassness. For this, some »strategic essentialism« (Spivak 1988: 13) had been necessary in sampling. The project's research perspective, nonetheless, distances itself strongly from an Islamic methodologism (Meer and Modood 2013) and does not intend to reify categories of difference or present Muslim youth as a distinct social actor with discrete action rationales based on religion. Young adults, Hindu or Muslim (and of other faiths) alike, are engaged in

---

71   Interestingly, academic research also tends to focus largely on Hindu middle class, e.g. Fernandes 2006, Varma 2007, Donner 2008, Donner/DeNeve 2011, Brosius 2010).

72   A Swiss National Fund supported project of the author. While within this larger project premarital relationships have been only one line of inquiry, this chapter draws, in the context of premarital relationships, on 104 ethnographic interviews (in Hindi/Urdu and English) with unmarried young men and women of the 18-30 age category who conceive themselves as Muslim and middle class. Within theoretical sampling (Glaser and Strauss 1967) »Muslim« and »middle class« were based on self-representation and were analysed as »categories of practice« (Brubaker and Cooper 2000: 4) subsequently. Moreover, social media content and Dating Apps were included in the analysis. In the following, pseudonyms have been used for all quoted interview sequences.

premarital relations (Ram et al. 2010: 200). The differences in attitudes toward premarital relations between generations thereby are bigger than differences between religious groups (ibid.). Being part of modern India, if not the »global cool«, and yearning for more autonomy with regard to romantic and sexual relations is part and parcel of young adults' everyday lives irrelevant of religious affiliation. Autonomy, lifestyle and sexuality have to be negotiated against (often) conflicting ideas of family elders (see e.g. Lukose 2009, Wessel 2011, Abraham 2002). The norms and morals that structure parental expectations often are perceived as tied to a particular religious community even though, as a Delhi court judgement (2014) has stated, premarital sex has to be considered as unmoral and against the tenets of every religion in India (Dutta and Dogra 2014). Generational negotiation processes thus are common to most young adults. However, they bear some special dynamics for Muslim youth. This has to do with the difference in which »*being a good Hindu*« and »*being a good Muslim*« relate to »*being Indian*«. The respective notions of what it means to be a 'good' Muslim by family norms, practices of everyday Islam, religious teachings, popular imaginaries of an Islamic modernity promoted by Tele-/*YouTube* Islam and ideas travelling through Middle East migrant networks, have to be aligned and reconciled with the need to repeatedly reaffirm legitimate national belonging (Hasan 2008).

Negotiating Field Relations, Mutual Stereotypes and Trust

A full methodological reflection on the researcher's positionality (female, 37-42 years old during fieldwork, foreign (gori), non-Muslim, a university teacher/researcher, a biker, etc.), consequent mutual expectations and the negotiation of power relations during fieldwork would easily make up a chapter on its own. Therefore only two points that seem to be central to situating the data discussed below will be briefly touched upon.

I had started fieldwork initially with married adults. When I began to go deeper into unmarried young adults' everyday practices and subsequently got interested in premarital relations, I realized how distant these practices are from their parents everyday life or rather from the parental generation as a whole. Even those parents who considered themselves really relaxed with their children having a boyfriend/girlfriend knew only the tip of the iceberg. Similarly, when I discussed some preliminary insights with colleagues at the University of Lucknow, their first reaction was disbelief. For one, because young Muslims were perceived to be more conservative, but also generally, the plus 40 years generation seemed to be out of tune with the changed realities in young adults love- and sex lives. The »western woman« (gori) stereotype and being a foreigner/outsider certainly helped in as much that my interview partners did not expect me to judge their dating and sexual practices as Indian adults of my age were assumed to do. Yet it also let to conversations in which I had to negotiate the expectation that I could assume the role of an »agony aunt«, i.e. to supportively give recommendations and tips with regard to dating based on my supposedly broad and longstanding experiences in that field. The same stereotype may also have encouraged in some cases exaggerated self-representations[73] to fulfil the presumed western woman's expectation of a normal love and sex life. Eventually, therefore, interpretations had to take into account boasting and maybe overreporting particularly by young men.[74] Despite the difficulties of negotiating expectations in my »Westerness«, over all I would say it constituted an advantage, both with regard to openness as well as the need to explicate experiences for an outsider.[75]

While any ethnographic research benefits from a setting of mutual *trust*, this seems to be even more needed when talking about intimate content like love, dating and sex. Since I mostly knew the parents and/or peers as well as sometimes the dating partners of my interviewees and other families in the respective neighbourhoods, this meant not just the trust in me dealing ethically with the data within my research project, but also the trust in my ability to handle my other »loyalties« in the field. While doing participant observation in various everyday contexts of the interviewees increased the significance of trust, it certainly also helped to build up this trust ongoingly

---

73   While at times, particularly in the beginning of setting up a research relation, some men may have misread the situation (despite the age gap) as flirty, only in two exceptional cases I eventually decided to abort further interaction because mutual expectations could not be cleared / a research relation comfortable for both, interviewer and interviewee could not be established. On sexual harassment and ethnographic fieldwork see e.g. Kloss 2017.

74   On the methodological problems of self-reporting sexual experiences, tendencies for male overreporting see e.g. Kelly et al. 2013, Clark et al. 2011.

75   Moreover, one has to keep in mind that self-representations are not just structured by the expectations towards the interviewer, but also by desirability according to dominant everyday discourses. As for instance men underlining manliness with virility and sexual experience or reproductions of the whore-virgin dilemma (McRobbie 2000), i.e. the link between chastity and female respectability (Gilbertson 2014, Yelvington 1999) as well as the related peer discourse in which women are less reprehensible and morally corrupted if they have sex in the context of love (Abraham 2002).

while negotiating research relations over several years of fieldwork. Obviously not all research relations were of the same intensity. But forging an (empathic) interest in one another (and for the research project), conversing, exchanging and explicating perspectives and experiences, discussing mutual gendered expectations and assumptions, spending time together usually intertwined the personal and professional (Murphy 2019) on the route of trying to achieve intersubjectivity. Friendly and emphatic, research relations are carefully established idiosyncratic relations that are constituted according to context by different forms of negotiating mutual expectations. They are distinct to »friendships« (Kirsch 2005) but also relations described in India in fictive kinship terms (e.g. *appi/didi*) as well as relations in which I would be addressed as »Madam« due to my age and my presence as academic researcher. To what extend mistrust (inhibitions as well as my informants' own projects) nonetheless may have shaped answers or what I was allowed to observe (participate in) eventually remains difficult to assess. As generally in ethnographic research, the field's representations and perspectives are polyphonic (Elwert 1994: 4), fractured and partial versions of »how things are or were«, and are competing with each other. Acknowledging and deliberately working with polyphone perspectives allows not only for contextualization, but also for the discovery of inconsistencies in the data or in individual evidence which provided particularly interesting points for subsequent inquiries.

Premarital Relationships

Young middle class Muslims in Lucknow continue to consider an arranged marriage as an unavoidable fact, the traditional appropriate way and as the religiously desired form of marriage.[76] Yet, dating and (heterosexual) premarital relations[77] are very much part of everyday young adult life in Lucknow. Having a girlfriend or boyfriend is not just the norm, but was talked about as constituting a crucial status marker within peer groups: »Only ugly

---

76 Survey data (HT-MaRS Youth Survey 2014) shows that the preference for arranged marriages is not specific to Muslim middle class youth, but that 98% of female and male respondents would prefer a religious to a court marriage (52% generally prefer an arranged marriage) and only 4% would marry against their parents objection.

77 To include queer/gay/lesbian premarital relations had been beyond the scope of this research project. For same-sex premarital relations, see e.g. Vanita 2013, Pandey/Mayuri 2013.

nerds do not have a girlfriend. If you do not manage to set at least one girl, you will be the joke of your friends!« (Bilal, m24).

> It's normal to have a boyfriend these days. Everybody has one. Even the most namazee [pious] girl will have some romantic relation with somebody. And for everybody else: if you have nobody in line [jo line mar raha] it means you're fat and ugly, (Bushra, f22)

However, in going about their premarital relationships, young adults accounted for two major, interrelated difficulties. Firstly, young adults stated that the guiding principle in their parental upbringing had been the cultural ideal »*tehzib*«,[78] i.e. »*utmost respectful interaction between women and men*« (Saif, m27), that often includes the demand to avoid any »*unnecessary interaction*« with the »*opposite sex*« (ibid.) outside kinship relations. Many young adults complained that consequently they lack in experiences in »*modern socializing*« as Nadeem (m28) for instance explains:

> The whole problem is very much due to Lucknow's tehzib culture. We are not allowed to communicate with the opposite sex. Lucknow's rules of respect force you into living in boys' and girls' worlds. There is no cultural model for appropriate interaction. The only appropriate way is no interaction.

While *tehzib* as ideal continues to structure interaction, and remnant forms of gender segregation are still in place in many public places over the last ten years also more liberal localities (cafés, restaurants, hookah lounges, etc.) have sprung up and are popular dating locations.[79] Secondly, despite these new mixed gender locations, young adults consider finding a private space for physical intimacy a big constraint. Unmarried Muslims usually live with their parents/relatives or in gender segregated hostels and student housing. Only male professionals who have no relatives in the city may have their own (or shared) apartments. Most young Muslims consider bringing their girlfriend/boyfriend/date home impossible. In very liberal families, who accepted their children bringing home a friend of the opposite sex, meeting at home still meant remaining under the watchful supervision of the parents in a common space of the house without privacy or at most to »*keep the door open at all times*«. Going on »joyrides« to isolated places is

---

78   *Tehzib* alludes to a particular Lucknawi lifestyle that refers above all to a certain code of conduct and form of interaction ruled by ideals of decency, politeness and respect. Originating from the historically rather short period of *Nawab* rule in Lucknow (Oudh, 1732-1818), the concept retains importance above all as an ideal, a source of pride, and feelings of belonging and heritage (Sharar, Llewellyn-Jones and Oldenburg 2001).

79   Campuses of the Universities and Colleges have been more liberal mix-gender spaces for a long time.

one way to avoid people's stares and comments (still bearing other risks) – but few young people have access to cars. It is understood to be the men's responsibility to provide a safe place to meet. Hence, young men already in salaried jobs may rent a room or small apartment on a shared basis among friends and then meet with their girl/friends there. In addition, alliances among friends to provide a space to meet in the absence of their parents may be another option. Whereas »*kissing and fondling is possible*« in the last row of movie theatres and in (some) Lucknow parks, »*for more privacy, one has to go to Kukrail Forest*« (Anzar, m23).[80] While a »park-date« is an option with young students, the older the couple gets, the more it has the bad taste of »*being poor or lower middle class*« (Sumaira, f25).

Technological Change and Dating

According to the narrative comparing »today« with »before«, two major watershed moments in dating were identified by (young) adults. Firstly, until the early 2000s, romantic relationships mostly started from actual face-to-face encounters and often remained without any physical intimacy (smiling at somebody on the road, exchanging letters). This is also what young people today perceive as the predominant dating practice of their parents' generation. The first major change happened with the emergence of internet cafés starting from 2000 onward. All of the sudden, it was possible to interact with a much wider set of people far beyond family, kinship, the close neighbourhoods or beyond immediate school/college contacts. Initially people interacted and extended their networks with the help of the very popular social media site Orkut, and then later started chatting via *yahoo/Hotmail* messenger. According to interviews, *Facebook ha* Pandian *s* constituted the most popular social media site since 2008.[81]

Secondly, the second turning point was the increasing proliferation of smart phones from 2010 onwards.[82] With »*the world in your pocket, from*

---

80   *Kukrail Forest* is a natural reserve on the outskirts of Lucknow. For an entry fee of 100 Rs (approx. 1.30 Euro) park guards guarantee that only couples can enter a particular area known as »*phase II*«.

81   For all Indian internet users *Facebook* ranks second after *YouTube* as the most popular social media website and *WhatsApp* ranks third in 2019 https://datare-portal.com/reports/digital-2019-india?rq=india (last accessed December 12, 2019).

82   All young middle class adults interviewed in Lucknow stated to have owned their first smartphone by the year 2013 at the latest. For comparison, according

porn to Zakir Naik«[83] (Sameera f25), young adults now have access to diverse transnational narratives of »coolness« and corresponding ideas about leisure activities, consumption desires as well as sexual possibilities. Young adults described the greatest change brought by smartphones in that they help to gauge the largely continuing barriers of interacting with each other, particularly with the other sex. With the saturation of smartphones in Lucknow around 2013, communication now theoretically is possible 24/7. Particularly for young Muslim women, whose mobility often is controlled by their families, the smartphone offers access to varied (alternative) social spaces by means of a new »media-communicative mobility« (Schneider 2015) – summed up by Sumaira (f24) as: *»I chat with my boyfriend, in fact with the world!! And that while I am lying in bed next to my sleeping daadi* [grandmother]*!«*

Contrary to the findings of Shoemaker (2015) in Pakistan, mobile phones and social media use in Muslim middle class families in Lucknow do not reproduce practices of *purdah*[84] in virtual spaces. All young middle class women interviewed had their own (»public«) *Facebook*[85] profile and used (»private«) *WhatsApp* at the same time. While *Facebook* is crucial for connecting with friends and new people, e.g. initiating a flirt, after some time young adults usually shift on to *WhatsApp* messenger for one-to-one communication. This shift in application also is symbolic in as much as it is conceived as mutual re-affirmation to carry on the initiated relation.

A second change often mentioned in the context of smartphones is the accessibility of porn. In interviews, both young men and women, highlighted that the availability of porn shaped expectations and attitudes towards premarital sex. They pointed to *»a real generation gap«* between those who had easy access to porn since early adolescence and those who were already above 25 years old when porn had reached their mobile phones. Both young women and men stated that the ubiquity of porn has contributed to considering premarital sex *»more normal«*. At the same time, they stated that it also increased the expectation that one actually has to have

---

to an all India survey 62% of all young adults (across all income groups, urban and rural) owned a personal smartphone in 2014 (Davey and Davey 2016: 1402).

83   A popular *YouTube* preacher, »the rock star of tele-evangelism and a proponent of modern Islam« (Rama 2016).

84   *Purdah* = lit. »curtain« refers to practices of gender segregation or even seclusion of women.

85   Some women kept their Facebook account with an alias name or had two profiles (one for family, one for a more daring self-representation) but this was common practice among young men as well.

sex before marriage (»*because everybody else apparently has!*«, Safraz, m20) and frustrations, where these expectations are not met.[86] Since 2014, in addition, dating apps *(Tinder, Truly Madly, OkCupid etc.)* have become increasingly popular. Because initiating first contact is perceived as a male responsibility[87], particularly young men stated to prefer dating apps, because they encourage confidence in approaching women:

> See this is what happens with the middle class Muslims. Our parents actually they scare us to death when you talk to a girl. They are like 'don't you dare to talk to girls!' This is how we are brought up. So we find it very difficult to face women, leave alone talk to them or ask them out (…) Latest thing I started trying is tinder. At least you know that all girls out there are singles [sic] and that they are eager to go on a date. When you get a match, you already know the girl thinks you look okay and that she has no problem dating a Muslim, (Rehman, m24).[88]

On the question why they are using a dating app like *tinder*, about a fourth of all male users interviewed reported that they are looking for »*a girlfriend*«, less than another fourth for »*hook-ups*« and the rest of users looked for what they called »*just friendship*«.[89] In contrast, none of the Muslim middle-class women interviewed said that they use dating apps to search for »*hook-ups*« and very few considered the app as a way to find a »*boyfriend*«. If at all, they as well, referred to »*just friendship*« as what they are looking for. Meeting up with their matches is an option only rarely exercised. Most young women were primarily interested in using dating apps as a convenient space »*to go out without going out*« (Seema, w22), i.e. to chat and flirt

---

86   Whereas interviewed men were eager to talk about watching porn, no women admitted to watching porn regularly. However, even women professing no interest in porn acknowledged that they had seen at least some clips »*out of curiosity*« or for »*educative purposes*«. But women unanimously stated that due to the availability of porn, »*guys are oversexed and desperate to do for themselves what they binge watch every day*« (Mariyem, f24) and that the pressure to agree to physical intimacy has increased.

87   Young women stated that they are aware of this unwritten rule, but they pointed out that they have their own (subtle) ways of making themselves visible (e.g. posting »replies« in timelines of friends) or that they even would initiate a conversation, but very rarely ask to be »added« as a friend, nor suggested to exchange phone numbers/shift to *WhatsApp*.

88   The (Muslim) name gives it away.

89   In contrast to singular »*hook-ups*«, »*just friends*«, refer to lasting, non-committed 'friends-with-benefits arrangements'. They come close to what Abraham (2002) summed up as »*time pass relations*«. However, while the colloquial »*time-pass*« expression has a negative connotation, the commonly deployed »*just friends*« analogy has a more neutral subtext and is used by both women and men to describe a relation they both define and negotiate.

from the safety of home, without having to to renegotiate physical mobility. Taking up a match and starting to chat were presented by both women and men as driven primarily by the curiosity in the other's (presumedly distant) lifeworld. This included a mutual interest to exchange views on sexual topics that may eventually lead to rather explicit chatting. Men acknowledged explicit chatting as core motivation to interact with their female online acquaintances. Women declared explicit content as »*something necessary to keep the boy interested*«, but mostly admitted to having fun in exploring sexual topics from the safety of their home.

Physical Intimacy, »Just Friendship« and Cross-Communal Dating

While women stated to opt for virtual relations and dating apps because they are possible even in conservative family settings, most young men were eager to eventually meet for »a real date«, as Azam (m24) explained:

> First, I flatter the girl and make her comfortable (...) when I have talked for a long time, I slowly lead things into a different genre (…) you get her into »truth or dare« and then I start asking naughty questions. This is how one gets her started (…) First you talk about private information, then you talk about private parts and then you start to meet her for private moments. That's the sequence.

Particularly for those relations that originated online, the courtship and the setting stage for physical intimacy usually takes place completely online. Young men and women are aware that premarital relations are against religious expectations, but at the same time, by stressing freedom and liberty, rationalized their own practices as an entitlement of being young.

> For me it [having premarital sex] is not haram [forbidden by the Quran]. I know it should be, but I can't help but consider sex something good. I am not very religious. I am a Muslim for sure. I do namaz [pray] at least twice a day. But I live in a modern world. And I want to consume it, live in it - not being caged in it! (…) If I eventually take on my parents' outdated mindset and marry a girl of their choice, I will do so after having enjoyed my youth to the fullest! I will save being a proper Muslim for after marriage, (Mohsab, m26).

However, virginity factors back in at the time of the arranged marriage when both families usually inquire in the respective future spouse's premarital life and moral immaculacy. Particularly for women chances to attract a good proposal at the time of marriage continue to be tied to her chastity (Chakraborty 2016). Consequently, in order to avoid dire consequences like a premature end to education or a hasty marriage, young women have to be extra careful that neither their parents nor other family members learn about their dating activities.[90] Not surprisingly, women generally feel more protective of their virginity. Women like Sadiya (f28) who boldly claims »*virginity is not my thing. Nothing to be proud of!*« are exceptional. While some women considered it rather "normal", and presented sex as something they enjoy and are entitled to for reasons of gender equality: »*if boys can have sex, why should we feel ashamed of doing the same?*« (Arifa, f22), most narratives downplayed sexual interest and did not portray women as the driving force in the process of initiating sex. Yet only five (out of 42) unmarried women interviewed eventually stated to never having had sex. The normative ambiguities expressed with regard to having sex usually were not presented as religions qualms and Shaheena's (f23) stance that

> I know that what I do is considered to be a sin and not good. But overall I do not think too much about it. I know that I am a Muslim and God will forgive me, even if I fail sometimes. (…) This is my youth!

could be seen as fairly typical. Instead of foregrounding religious reservations, most women stated that they rather worry about being perceived as »*too easy*« or being labelled as »*sluts*« or »taxi« (»*who gives a lift to anybody*«) by young men and within their peer group.

Romantic/committed relationships do exist, but a large share of dating in Lucknow is very casual. Moreover, despite the public discourse(s) that perpetuates negative stereotypes of the respective other community (which is reproduced by young adults in some contexts) a great part of dating in Lucknow is in fact inter-communal. Without exception, everybody interviewed had also dated Hindus. Some stated that »*at this point in our life, religion does not matter when it comes to relationships, we just have fun*«. *(Quayam, m25)* or that it had happened rather coincidentally for »*if you get attracted to somebody, it is not to his religion, but to him as a person*« (Umaira, f22). Others pointed out that it had been a more conscious decision along the lines of »*Hindu girls are more easy going* [open to sexual intimacy]« (m) or because »*Hindu boys are less judgemental*« (f). Both women and men stated that intercommunal relations are »*easier because nobody expects marriage*« since for the majority of inter-communal relations it is clear from the beginning that they are set up for a specific time and that it is a relation »*lived in the moment*« (Hasan, m24). Dating Hindus thus has nothing to do with a »*love-jihad*«, i.e. converting Hindus by marriage to Islam, as often accused by the Hindu Right (Gupta 2009). Even if some young women (and

---

90   Many young women, in order to stay incognito, wear a version of hijab that covers most of their face or even a *burqa* when meeting with their dates in a place they rather do not wish to be seen by relatives - even if otherwise they do not wear *hijab*.

men) keep a distant hope for a »*love-marriage*«, by and large they are more than aware that (particularly cross-communal) dating, »*has nothing to do with marriage*«.

Processes of Distinction: Middleclassness and Dating

Several studies suggest that youth and young adults of lower income segments are pioneering premarital relations in number of relationships and age at first sexual experience (Ram et al. 2010, Singh et al. 2014, Chakraborty 2016 for dating among Muslim slum-dwellers). This starkly contrasts with perceptions of those young adults in Lucknow who position themselves as Muslims and middle class. Without exception, all participants of the research project were convinced that low economic status and strict adherence to religious norms coincide. They portrayed dating as an urban middle class or upper middle class phenomenon. They substantiated this evaluation with »their own observations«. They based the latter primarily on middle class youth culture that loudly stages itself in social media, or on the popular Hindi cinema that presents premarital (sexual) relations as an upper middle class phenomenon. Furthermore, premarital relationships are considered part and parcel of Western, »modern« youth culture – of which young adults are aware through movies, music, media, *YouTube* and social media. Consequently, many young adults presented their own dating practices (or aspirations) inspired by what they thought they know about middle class youth practices in Delhi and Bombay or for that matter in London or elsewhere in the global North. At the same time, the everyday life of economically marginalised (Muslim) young adults takes place in socially distant and less medialized social spaces. Young middle class adults had only very vague and stereotypical ideas about urban poor, despite poor neighbourhoods or slums being situated very close to their own residential areas. They constructed their own lifestyles as different from those of poor Muslims, whom they portray as »*conservative*«, »*traditional*«, »*backward*«, »*ignorant*«, »*much more religious*«, or even »*religiously zealous*«.

In addition to explaining the alleged absence of dating among poor or lower middle class young adults with supposedly a more orthodox morality, they are also convinced that youth of lower income groups lack the cultural capital (style, manners, etc.) and subcultural codes needed to move confidently in spaces associated with middle-class dating culture. The construction of dating as embodied middleclassness was further substantiated by pointing out how expensive dating, corresponding self-fashioning and securing a private space for physical intimacy are. The underlying assumption being that poor/lower middle class Indians financially just could not embrace dating even if they would want to.

In representing dating as synonymous with being »middle-class« and being »modern« young adults thus distinguish themselves simultaneously from the lower classes, the conservative moral discourse of their parental generations as well as the dispositive of the »orthodox, backward Muslim«. The distinction from the »backward Muslim« is particularly interesting since they do not categorically reject the essentialist stereotype. In a process of revisiting the practice of othering (Said 1978), it merely is inscribed to »the Muslim poor«, i.e. a Muslim other »Other«.

Conclusion: Situative Plural Affiliations of Belonging

Technological change, especially the immediate access to social and communicative media with the proliferation of smartphones has created new possibilities of getting in contact with a larger and more diversified set of people. As a consequence new interfaces of otherwise distant gendered social spaces including their diverse social stocks of knowledge have emerged. The access to social media offers new possibilities for self-representation and visibility, but above all they bridge still existing gendered constraints of women and men approaching and interacting with each other in Lucknow. Moreover, technological change has created alternative (virtual/imagined) spaces and opportunities for »transformational play« (Whitty and Carr 2003). Alternative practices, challenging societal ideals of femininity/masculinity and related notions of respectability have become possible at least within these imagined spaces. »Self-realization through intimacy« (Giddens 1992) - and be it virtual - opens avenues to exploring alternative subjectivities and sexualities. Yet, expanding »networks of intimacy« (Pertierra 2005: 43) do not necessarily mean changes in actual physical mobility or renegotiation of gender or generational relations. Intimate virtual and romantic/physical relations take place primarily »back stage« (Löw 2003) in virtual or rather clandestine social spaces. Thus, particularly young women's agency in making sexual choices and exploring their sexualities often continues to depend on keeping the matter private.

Dating, despite these limits, nonetheless constitutes an interface in which conflicting sets of norms, ideas about masculinity, femininity, sexuality, autonomy, global youth culture, peer group expectations, and multiple belongings are getting negotiated. Young Muslim men and women, are both more than aware that their actual practices conflict with religious norms. However, the majority did not portray ambivalences as unbearable or a burden to their conscience. Nor did they suffer from an internal diremption of »segmented identities« (Pries 1996). Rather they considered their own practices as meaningful and not overly contradictive. They portrayed liberty and autonomy as achievements of modernity they felt entitled to. They made sense of their actions by prioritizing personal »freedom« (autonomy), their own desires and the wish to be part of a modern youth culture over religious directives. While they consider childhood as regulated by parents and married life by family obligations, »youth« is constructed as the phase of life when one is entitled to freedom and exploration. Ideas about entitlements and self-realisation but also yearning for roots and belonging are disentangled by assigning different spatial (home/family/*khandan*) and temporal (after youth/after marriage) frames to »being a good Muslim«. By not challenging the arranged marriage ideal, but keeping dating disassociated from marriage, they are able to partly reconcile conflicting norms while making the most of their current situation. Whereas this spatial-temporal separation has been foregrounded in narratives, it could be above all an attempt to rationalize their practices. When it comes to everyday life being »Muslim«, »Indian«, »middle class«, »*cool*« and »*modern*« are not binaries or mutually exclusive, but seem to be rather dissolved in »transcultural« (Welsch 2010) practices. Even if conflicting sets of norms and values prompted some youth to complain that they »*feel somehow lost in transition*« (Ali, m21) and under great pressure to make the right choices, most young people had a rather hands-on, contextual approach towards the many new opportunities and possibilities. They overcame the trade-offs of transition for instance by considering themselves »grey Muslims«. By this, they meant that »*at times white and pure*« as in regularly going to the mosque / praying and discursively endorsing religious norms, and »*at other times being on the dark, haram side*« with hanging out in cafes and hookah lounges, wasting their money on »cool« consumer goods (»*worshipping the goods in the malls*«), dating, having sex, or even drinking alcohol. Most of the time, however, they would be »*grey as in invisible, like everybody else*« (Tariq, m25).

Thereby, feeling part of a common Indian youth culture (*»grey as everybody else«*) is constructed primarily on the idea of being »modern«. [91]

Apart from discussing dating practices and the renegotiation of mobility particularly in virtual spaces in the context of technological change, this chapter showed how young Muslims relate dating to aspiration and how dating practices are used in processes of negotiating the boundaries of middleclass membership and self-positioning with respect to »modern India«. It has been argued that dating and its construction as embodied middleclassness offers a counter-narrative to »backwardness« and creates further dimensions of belonging as well. The latter are generated by specific peer-group- and translocal youth-cultures that are articulated in different social (virtual and nonvirtual) spaces. Economic and cultural resources allow for more diverse, ambivalent and flexible positionings and varied strategies to resolve conflicting (generational) expectations and to negotiate varied sets of norms and values. While in everyday practices binary categories are being dissolved, permeate each other or are drawn from selectively, temporarily and situatively, they simultaneously are ascribed and maintained by being passed on to others (Muslim poor/Muslim lower middle class) in these very processes of distinction and self-positioning.

References

Abraham L. (2002). »Bhai-Behen, True Love, Time Pass: Friendships and Sexual Partnerships among Youth in an Indian Metropolis«. *Culture, Health & Sexuality*, 3: 337-53.

Amin, Shahid (2005). »Representing the Musalman: Then and Now, Now and Then«. In: Mayaram, Shail, Pandian, M.S.S. and Skaria, Ajai (Eds.). *Muslims, Dalits and the Fabrications of History. Subaltern Studies XII.* New Delhi: Permanent Black. 1-35.

Bhandari, Parul (2017). »Pre-marital Relationships and the Family in Modern India«. *Samaj* 16: 1-20.

Brosius, Christiane (2010). *India's Middle Class: New Forms of Urban Leisure. Consumption and Prosperity.* London: Routledge.

Brubaker, Rogers and Cooper, Frederick (2000). Beyond Identity. *Theory and Society* 29.1: 1-47.

Chacko, Priya (2018). »Marketizing Hindutva: The State, Society, and Markets in Hindu Nationalism«. *Modern Asian Studies.* 1-34.

---

91   This includes a fascination with technological progress, certain consumer goods, fashion statements and fluid lifestyle options, merit-based employment opportunities and promises of economic upward mobility, the valuation of autonomy and individual fulfilment, including romantic and sexual premarital experiences.

Chakraborty, Kabita (2016). *Young Muslim Women in India. Bollywood, Identity and Changing Youth Culture.* London: Routledge.

Clark, Shelley; Karibu, Caroline, and Zulu,Eliya (2011). »Do Men and Women Report Their Sexual Partnerships Differently?« *International Perspectives on Sexual and Reproductive Health* 37(4): 181-90.

Davey, Sanjeev and Davey, Anuradha (2016). »Assessment of Smartphone Addiction in Indian Adolescents: A Mixed Method Study by Systematic-review and Meta-analysis Approach«. *International Journal of Preventive Medicine* 5(12): 1500-1511.

Donner, Henrike (2008). *Domestic Goddesses: Maternity, Globalization and Middle-Class Identity in Contemporary India.* New York: Routledge.

---. and De Neeve, Geert (2011). »Introduction«. In: Donner, Henrike and Geert De Neve. *Being Middle Class in India.* London: Routledge. 1-22.

Dutta, Jayanti and Dogra, Meenakshi (2014). »Exploring Young People Perspective on Premarital Sex in India«. *The International Journal of Humanities & Social Studies*, 2(11): 44-51.

Fernandes, Leela (2006). *India's New Middle Class: Democratic Politics in an Era of Economic Reform.* Minneapolis: University of Minnesota Press.

Government of India (2010). »Romance and Sex Before Marriage among Young Women and Men in India«. *Youth in India: Situation and Needs, Policy Brief* 34. New Delhi: Government of India.

--- (2011). *Census of India.* New Delhi: Government of India.

Giddens, Anthony (1992). *The Transformation of Intimacy: Sexuality, Love, and Eroticism in Modern Societies.* Stanford: Stanford University Press.

--- (2014). »A Fine Balance: Negotiating Fashion and Respectable Femininity in Middle-Class Hyderabad, India«. *Modern Asian Studies* 48(1): 120-158.

Glaser, Barney G. and Strauss, Anselm L.(1967). *The Discovery of Grounded Theory: Strategies for Qualitative Research.* New York: Aldine de Gruyter.

Gupta, Charu (2009). »Hindu Women, Muslim Men: Love Jihad and Conversions«. *Economic and Political Weekly.* December 19, XLIV(51): 13-15.

Hasan, Mushirul (2008). *Moderate or Militant: Images of India's Muslims.* New Delhi: Oxford University Press.

Hasnain, Syed Iqbal (2009). *Muslims in India: Frozen in the Past.* New Delhi: Har-Anand.

HT-MaRS (2014). Youth Survey. *Young, Conservative, Traditional: Here's India's Gennext.* http://www.hindustantimes.com/india/young-conservative-traditional-here-s-india-s-gen-next/story-cRTMs9zgwqcBGOdlde6s1I.html (last accessed December 11, 2019).

HT-MaRS (2015). *Youth Survey.* http://projects.hindustantimes.com/ht-mars-youth-survey-2015 (last accessed April 22, 2016, the source is no longer available).

Kelly, Christine A. et al. (2013). »Social Desirability Bias in Sexual Behavior Reporting: Evidence from an Interview Mode Experiment in Rural Malawi«. *International Perspectives on Sexual and Reproductive Health* 39(1): 14-21.

Krishnan, Sandhya and Neeraj Hatekar (2017). »Rise of the New Middle Class in India and Its Changing Structure«. *Economic & Political Weekly* 3(22): 40-48.

Kirsch, Gesa E. (2005). »Friendship, Friendliness, and Feminist Fieldwork«. *Signs* 30(4): 2163–2172.

Löw, Martina (2003). *Raumsoziologie*. Frankfurt a.M.: Suhrkamp.

Lukose, Ritty (2009). *Liberalization's Children: Gender, Youth, and Consumer Citizenship in Globalizing India*. Durham: Duke University Press.

Marcus, George E. (1998). »Ethnography through Thick and Thin« In: George E. Marcus. *Ethnography in/of the World System: The Emergence of Multi-Sited Ethnography*. Princeton: Princeton Univ. Press. 79-104.

McRobbie, Angela (2000). *Feminism and Youth Culture*. Houndmills, Basingstoke: Macmillan.

Meer, Nasar and Tariq Modood (2013). »Beyond 'Methodological Islamism'? A Thematic Discussion of Muslim Minorities in Europe«. *Advances in Applied Sociology* 3(7): 307–313.

Misra, Amalendu (2004). *Identity and Religion: Foundations of Anti-Islamism in India*. New Delhi: Sage.

MRDA (2010). *India Today Group Sex Survey. Women Want More*. New Delhi: India Today. https://www.indiatoday.in/india-today-sex-survey/406176-2012-12-12 (last accessedJune 2016, the source is no longer available).

Murphy, Fiona (2019). »Friend or Foe?: A Reflection on the Ethno-Politics of Friendship and Ethnographic Writing in Anthropological Practice«. *Etnofoor* 31(1): 11–28.

Osella, Caroline and Filippo Osella (1998). »Friendship and Flirting: Micro-Politics in Kerala, South India«. *The Journal of the Royal Anthropological Institute* 4 (2): 189-206.

Pandey, Alka and K. Mayuri (2013). »Emerging Adult's Perception on Romantic Love, Homosexuality and Pre Marital Sexual Relationship«. *Research Journal of Recent Sciences* 2: 296-303.

Pertierra, Raul (2005): »Mobile Phones, Identity and Discursive Intimacy«. *Human Technology* 1(1): 23-44.

Pries, Ludger (1996). »Transnationale soziale Räume. Theoretisch-empirische Skizze am Beispiel der Arbeitswanderungen Mexiko – USA«. *Zeitschrift für Soziologie* 25(6): 456-772.

Ram, Usha et al. (2010). *Youth in India: Situation and Needs. Government of India Report. International Institute for Population Sciences*. New Delhi: Population Council.

Said, Edward (1978). *Orientalism*. New York: Pantheon Books.

Schneider, Nadja-Christina (2015). »Applying the Lens of Mobility to Media and Gender Studies. An Introduction« In: Nadja-Christina Schneider and Carola Richter (Eds.). *New Media Configurations and Socio-Cultural Dynamics in Asia and the Arab World*. Baden-Baden: Nomos. 222-241.

Sharar, Abdul Halim; Llewellyn-Jones , Rosie and Oldenburg, Veena Talwar (Eds.) (2001). *The Lucknow Omnibus: Lucknow the Last Phase of an Oriental Culture/a*

Fatal Friendship: The Nawabs, the British and the City of Lucknow/the Making of Colonial Lucknow 1856. New Delhi: Oxford University Press.

Shoemaker, Emrys (2015). 'Digital Purdah'. How Gender Segregation Persists over Social Media. *Dawn.* http://www.dawn.com/news/1197345 (last accessed December 11, 2019).

Simpson, Kathryn (2008). *Gifts, Markets and Economies of Desire in Virginia Woolf.* Basingstoke: Palgrave.

Spivak, Gayatri Chakravorty (1988). »Subaltern Studies: Deconstructing Historiography«. In: Gayatri Chakravorty Spivak and Ranajit Guha (Eds.). *Selected Subaltern Studies.* New York: Oxford University Press. 3– 32.

Uberoi, Patricia (2011). »The Sexual Character of the Indian Middle Class: Sex Surveys, Past and Present«. In: Amita Baviskar and Raka Ray (Eds.). *Elite and Everyman: The Cultural Politics of the Indian Middle Class.* New Delhi: Routledge. 271-299.

Welsch, Wolfgang (2010). »Was ist eigentlich Transkulturalität?« In: Lucyna Darowska, Thomas Lüttenberg and Claudis Machold (Eds.). *Hochschule als transkultureller Raum? Kultur, Bildung und Differenz in der Universität.* Bielefeld: Transcript. 39–66.

Wessel, Margit van (2011). »Cultural Contractions and Intergenerational Relations: The Construction of Selfhood Among Middle Class Youth in Baroda«. In: Henrike Donner (Ed.). *Being Middle Class in India.* London: Routledge. 100-116.

Whitty, Monica T. and Adrian N. Carr (2003). »Cyberspace as Potential Space: Considering the Web as a Playground to Cyber-Flirt«. *Human Relations* 56(7): 861-891.

Vanita, Ruth (Ed.) (2013). *Queering India: Same-Sex Love and Eroticism in Indian Culture and Society.* New York: Routledge.

Varma, Pavan K. (1998). *The Great Indian Middle Class.* New Delhi: Viking.

Yelvington, K. A. (1999). »Power/Flirting«. *The Journal of the Royal Anthropological Institute* 5(3): 457–60.

List of Contributors

PARUL BHANDARI is a sociologist and Associate Professor at the Jindal Global Business School in Sonipat. Her research interests include the study of social class, family, marriage, gender, media and popular culture, and money. She completed her PhD from the University of Cambridge, UK, in 2014. She is the author of three books: *Matchmaking in Middle Class India: Beyond Arranged and Love Marriage* (Springer 2020); *Money, Culture, Class: Elite Women as Modern Subjects*, (Routledge, 2019). She occasionally writes in popular outlets including Scroll.in, The Print, and The Conversation.

NADJA-CHRISTINA SCHNEIDER is Professor in Gender and Media Studies for the South Asian Region. Her areas of interest include Area Media Studies, Gender and Mobility Studies and Urban Studies. She has worked and published on the role of the Indian press in the context of the Shah Bano case and the subsequent debate on Muslim Personal Law; on the development of the Indian media system and changing media environments in post-liberalization India; documentary filmmakers working on Gender and Islam and on the emergence of Delhi as a cinematic city.

STEFANIE STRULIK holds an MA in Sociology and a PhD in Social Anthropology and is a research fellow at the Geneva Graduate Institute (IHEID), Department of Anthropology and Sociology in Switzerland. She has been working ethnographically in Northern India for the last 25 years. Her research interests include the gendered social embeddeness of politics, local democracy, competing narratives of modernity, middle class as politicized cultural project(s), gender and religious nationalism.

FRITZI-MARIE TITZMANN is Assistant Professor in Modern South Asian Studies at Leipzig University. She was a visiting professor at the Cross-Sectional Department of Gender and Media Studies for the South Asian Region (Institute of Asian and African Studies, Humboldt-Universität zu Berlin) in the summer term of 2019. Her research focuses on gender, media, and social change in contemporary India. She has published on the Indian online matrimonial market, including a monograph (2014, in German), social activism, sexuality and media representations.